Bones, Shells, and Curios

A CONTEMPORARY METHOD OF CASTING THE BONES

written and illustrated by
MICHELE JACKSON

Lucky Mojo Curio Company
Forestville, California

↭ 2014 ↭

Bones, Shells, and Curios:
A Contemporary Method of Casting the Bones
by Michele Jackson

© 2014 Michele Jackson

Text:
Michele Jackson

Editors:
catherine yronwode and Deacon Millett

Cover:
Michele Jackson and Greywolf Townsend

Illustrations:
Michele Jackson

Production:
Deacon Millett, nagasiva yronwode, Greywolf Townsend

First Edition 2014
Second Edition 2017

Published by
The Lucky Mojo Curio Company
6632 Covey Road
Forestville, California 95436
LuckyMojo.com

ISBN: 978-0-9719612-7-2

Printed in Canada.

TABLE OF CONTENTS

DEDICATION

This book is dedicated to my husband Leroy and my daughter Elena. You have both supported and indulged me in all of my many interests and enthusiasms, no matter how unorthodox or strange they seemed to you.

ACKNOWLEDGMENTS

First I would like to thank my mother Frances Askin, who taught me to read at the age of four and taught me to love knowledge and learning.

Chas Bogan of The Mystic Dream gave me my first bone reading and was the source of some techniques that I use today.

catherine yronwode, the co-proprietress of the magical Lucky Mojo Curio Company, sold me my first set of sangoma-style bones and spent much of her valuable time that day showing me how to use them. She and her husband nagasiva have been instrumental in bringing this book to publication by Lucky Mojo.

Deacon Millett graciously volunteered to help with layout and formatting, a task I found much more difficult than writing. This book would not have been be possible without him.

Thanks also to Greywolf Townsend for his cover design and to Professor Charles Porterfield and Phoenix LeFae for help with proofreading the final manuscript.

Thanks to Kast Excelsior, Bonemaster Ka, for allowing me to reproduce his reading cloth.

Gretchen Crilly McKay, shaman and sangoma at Ancestral Wisdom, whose talent and teaching skills allowed me to let go and let spirit guide my readings. Some of the techniques she taught me are in this book.

I would also like to thank L. Cook, J. Jensen, G. Pita, N. Grantham, A. C. Bogan and K. Campbell, the students in my first bone reading class. I learned more from you than I taught you. I am grateful to those clients who gave me their permission for their readings to be used in this book.

I would also like to thank God, the forces of nature, and my ancestors and spirits for leading me to this path. Nothing would be possible without them.

INTRODUCTION

Recently bone reading has become more visible and popular in the United States. While it has always been visible in some parts of the world like South Africa, in the U.S. it has mostly been the province of healers and rootworkers in the South. It seemed to be dying out, but a revival of sorts is taking place as more people become interested in hoodoo, conjure, and shamanism.

Bone reading requires and reinforces a connection with one's ancestors. Regardless of culture or style of reading, the ancestor connection in this type of divination is evident.

Our modern culture is fast paced and it highlights and celebrates the individual over the group. We are so busy that we often find it hard to take a few moments to sit in meditation. Many of us are so stressed with work, paying the bills, finding time to spend with those we love, and just getting through the day that we scarcely give more than an occasional thought in passing to those who went before us.

However, I think we are going to see a shift. Now more than ever the ancestors are calling out to us. Classes and courses in working with the ancestors and healing ancestral issues are starting to be much more available and, via the internet, quite easily accessible.

I think there is a yearning and a need in our society to look back as well as forward and to commune with and acknowledge those who came before and made our current lives possible. Bone reading is an excellent tool for doing this type of work.

I also believe that if you are reading this book you may have been drawn to bone reading at the urging of your ancestors. If you know that is the reason you are reading this book, then good for you! This method will probably work well for you since your ancestors are eager to communicate with you this way and they are making it known.

But even if you are just looking at this book because you liked the cover, I encourage you to set up an ancestor altar and give thanks to those who came before you, even if you find that this method isn't for you or if you never pick up the bones.

I have been a diviner for all of my adult life. I got my first tarot deck at age 16, I ran a hugely successful tarot web site, and I have even created several decks of my own. I will always have a deep love and respect for the tarot. However, since working with the bones, they have become my divinatory method of choice.

I came to this type of bone reading via hoodoo and conjure, but I bought my first set of divination bones many years ago. I don't even remember where I bought the set, but it was a little bag of bones and stones from South Africa, probably made for the tourist trade. It had a small fold out card with instructions and I tried it for a bit, but I was never able to make much sense of it.

I still have that set, but the bones have dried out and cracked and have taken on the color of the dyed pouch they came in. More recently, but still many years ago, I purchased a set of Mongolian shaggai in a beautifully embroidered bag that had been brought here from Mongolia. This is a divination system and a game that uses four sheep knuckles. I played with this set a bit as well, but I never considered them a serious replacement for my tarot cards.

I saw my first set of sangoma style bones while I was staying with friends who were sponsoring a tarot class that I was giving. My first night at their home I was given my first bone reading. The bone set was beautiful and the reading was dead on accurate. I knew that this was a method of divination that I wanted to try. I bought my first set of bones the very next day. I was fortunate enough to be given encouragement and advice at the time I bought that set. I was advised at the beginning to acquire additional pieces to expand the basic set, and several approaches to throwing the bones were demonstrated to me in person. I tried all of the approaches demonstrated to me that day over time before finally settling on my current method.

My first attempts at reading were often frustrating, but I got amazing readings often enough to keep me from giving up. My turning point came when I found and took lessons from a sangoma and shaman who is a professional reader. She gently helped me to let go of the highly structured approach I had brought to bone reading from my years of tarot reading. With her guidance and encouragement I was emboldened to allow spirit to guide me in my readings.

I also spent a lot of time practicing and swapping readings with other bone readers, both fledgling and professional. I can honestly say that I learned something from every bone reading I have ever gotten from another reader, no matter what their level of skill or experience.

I hope this book gives you the information you need to get started and the impetus to try your hand at bone reading and to work with your ancestors.

ABOUT THIS BOOK

My goal for this book is to give you an introduction to a contemporary bone reading method and to provide you with enough information to get you started. I can teach you how *I* read the bones, but I cannot teach you how *you* read the bones.

Bone readers are spirit led — guided by their Gods, their ancestors, and the spirits they work with. Add to this personal gnosis and everyday life experience, and you see that it would be impossible for any two bone readers to read alike.

This book is only a guide. It provides information that I learned from embodied teachers and from spirit, from books, from workshops, and through good old trial and error. My hope is to give you the information that you need to get started and to reduce the frustration that always accompanies learning a new skill, especially a spiritually-based skill.

Nothing you read here, study from another book, or learn from other readers will substitute for developing a relationship with your ancestors and the spirits. Nothing will substitute for time spent doing readings for yourself and others. But if you develop those relationships and put in time practicing and reading, I think that you will find this method of divination rewarding on many levels.

The method presented here is not derived solely from historical traditions. It draws upon older methods of bone casting, but at the same time is contemporary and unique. In order to help you understand what is being presented here, I will start by explaining what this form of contemporary bone reading is not.

First, this is not a traditional hoodoo or conjure-style bone reading, like those practiced in the Southern United States. Those styles are usually done by casting the bones of one species of animal, most often a chicken or a possum. The reader may also include dominoes or dice.

Hoodoo-style bone reading employs far fewer bones than this method, and the style of interpretation is different as well. In a Southern-style bone reading, the diviner usually interprets the cast bones with respect to their assigned meanings (for instance a chicken bone signifies travel) and by considering their position on an imagined or drawn-out circle, which may or may not be divided into quarters. Against the backdrop of the circle and its allotted areas, the patterns formed by the bones tell the narrative of the divination.

This is also not a mathematically-based system of bone reading, like the African hakata, which uses four symbolically-carved cattle rib bones, or the Mongolian shaggai, which employs four astragalus bones, typically from a sheep.

Hakata and shaggai are ancient forms of bone reading, but functionally speaking, they are quite similar to other casting methods like African obi and diloggun that utilize nuts, or cut cowrie shells, or other systems in which the marker-pieces are bone dice, dominoes, yarrow stalks, or coins.

Mathematical bone casting systems have fixed outcomes. Depending on the method used, the possibilities will range from 5 - 256 in number and good readers will memorize all of the possibilities. Not so in our method.

Finally, this is not a sangoma reading style, although to the observer it may resemble a sangoma reading, because the bones of several species, mingled with shells, carvings and curios, are thrown on a mat and are interpreted holistically.

Sangomas are the traditional healers and shamans of their communities in South Africa and bone reading is just one piece of a wide ranging skill set that they possess. Their skills are interdependent.

People usually go to the sangoma when they are physically ill or spiritually troubled and they are usually prescribed herbs and medicines to be used to heal the condition. The bone reading is just one part of the healing modality of a professional sangoma, and learning how to read bones "sangoma style" will not make you a sangoma.

The information presented here is intended as just a jumping-off point. As you start to work with the bones and with your ancestors you may receive guidance that is different from what is presented here. My advice is to follow the guidance that you receive from spirit.

This book contains no dogma. It doesn't describe "the right way" to read bones, either for yourself or for clients. It merely describes how I read the bones for myself and for my clients.

My hope is that what you find here will assist you in getting started as a bone reader and that getting started will re-connect you with your ancestors or deepen your connection if you are already working with them. In today's fast paced, troubled world their advice is sorely needed.

For more information about worldwide bone reading systems of many types, see the book *Throwing the Bones: How to Foretell the Future with Bones, Shells, and Nuts* by catherine yronwode.

WORKING WITH THE ANCESTORS

This is a brief introduction to working with the ancestors. I believe that bone reading requires a relationship with the ancestors and that working with the ancestors is not something that you hear much about in our secular culture.

Many books exist on the subject and most spiritual practitioners can give guidance in ancestral work within their traditions. If you are working within a spiritual tradition, please seek guidance from your own community on working with the ancestors. You will likely receive a much more in-depth means of practice than provided here. I have written what follows for those who are not working within a particular tradition, or whose religious training and upbringing has not included communion with or veneration of ancestral spirits.

THE ANCESTOR ALTAR

The easiest way that I know to begin a relationship with the ancestors is to erect an ancestor altar and use it regularly to meditate and communicate with your ancestors. This need not be a large, elaborate affair — it can be a small space on a dresser top, a shelf, or a side table. The space should be in a part of the house where you can sit quietly and meditate undisturbed.

The area should be kept free of clutter to the extent possible as a sign of respect. That said, the ancestors know your situation and will understand that space may be at a premium and that life is sometimes messier than we would like. Making the effort and showing respect is more important than having a huge space and keeping the area white glove ready.

When setting up a sacred space, what objects are present can be as important as the location you choose. Pictures of your ancestors, small mementos that belonged to them if you have them, a white candle, and a glass of water are a good beginning.

You can add flowers if you like and the occasional shot of strong spirits is also appreciated if they drank in life and did not have any issues with alcohol abuse or addiction. If they preferred coffee or tea, then offer them those to drink. Tobacco is another common gift, if they were smokers. Food, wrapped candies, and seasonal items from nature, such as bright autumn leaves or sand from a beach that they loved to visit, are also good offerings. If it would make a loving gift in life, it is appropriate for the altar.

Unless you belong to a religious tradition that places strictures or rules on how adherents must and must not create ancestor altars you will be able to make your own decisions regarding the altar's size, where it is situated, and what offerings are to be placed upon it. You can also choose for yourself whether it is intended for public viewing, is tucked away in a private area, or is "hidden in plain sight" by being integrated in an unassuming shelf or cabinet.

The key point is that the area should be used to talk to the ancestors and to re-establish a relationship with them if you do not currently have one. I say re-establish because it is my belief that they have always had a relationship with you, whether you were aware of it or not.

If you have not worked with ancestors in the past, your ancestor altar is a good place to re-establish your side of the relationship. Try to spend time at your altar daily. Tell your ancestors about your day, about your troubles, about your triumphs and challenges. Ask them for their guidance and assistance.

Just as you love your family and want to see them do well and succeed. the ancestors are also your family and they want the same thing for you. Make them a part of your life, express gratitude for their sacrifices on your behalf, and thank them and reward them if you feel they have helped you in some way.

I store my bones and reading cloths either on or near my ancestor altar, depending on how much space is available. This way, they are always under their protection and influence when I am not using them. To me the bones and the ancestors are inextricable.

Why is this important? Because this method of bone reading relies on ancestral guidance. In my research on various bone reading methods, one common thread was that it was not the diviner doing the reading, but the ancestors, spirits, or deity doing the divination.

The diviner is interpreting what the ancestors and spirits are saying. Some believe the ancestors and spirits are speaking through the diviner and some believe that they are speaking through the bones themselves, but either way the ancestors and spirits are the source — and your relationship with them has a vital role to play.

In my own work I start every reading by calling on God and the ancestors. I also call on the spirits that I work with. I use a rattle and bells while requesting their presence. While calling and rattling and ringing, at some point I can feel a slight shift in the energy that tells me that I am ready to read.

Having done ancestor work before I ever tried to read the bones, I found this divination method to be a natural fit. However, if you have not been working with your ancestors, you might want to start doing so. Establishing and maintaining an ancestor altar is the first place to start. Will this method of divination work without a connection to spirit or the ancestors? I don't know. But even if you can read without a connection to your ancestors, I think a good relationship with the ancestors and spirit can only enhance both your life and your readings.

WHERE TO GET A SET OF BONES

This method is similar to a sangoma reading in that it contains bones from more than one species, as well as a variety of shells and curios. There are several ways to acquire such a set of bones.

THE STARTER SET OF BONES

The easiest way to acquire bones is to order a set from a vendor. A list of sources is provided at the end of this book. Bone sets as currently sold are what I call "starter sets," and they are usually labeled as such. You will receive several bones and other pieces to get you started. Individual readers personalize their sets by adding different items. In fact, every reader I know has added something to the basic set.

Another way to acquire a set of bones is to gather the pieces you need from scratch. Several shops carry a variety of animal bones and curios. You can even procure entire skeletons. Those who spend time outdoors may come across bones already cleaned by nature. It can be difficult to determine the source species for found bones, but occasionally the skeleton is complete enough for the species to be identified. If knowing the species is important to you it may be best to buy bones from a reputable dealer.

THE CONTAINER

You will need some type of container for your bones when they are not in use. Some online vendors sell containers, such as large abalone shells, baskets, or boxes, but you can find one locally as well. I use a basket with a lid for my main set and I use the basket lid to toss the bones onto the cloth. I use a smaller basket for my travel set. It also has a lid, but I throw this set from the basket itself.

Any type of small container that you find aesthetically pleasing can be used. I prefer natural materials. I have used a carved wooden bowl with a lid for a container. I have seen readers who use ceramic containers and readers who use baskets without a lid. I have seen readers who store their bones in the cloth bag their starter set came in.

Use anything you feel is suitable and attractive and if you find that you can cast from it as well, so much the better.

Whichever container you choose should be cleansed to the extent possible, as will be described later. Likewise any portable reading surface you decide to use should be cleansed.

EXTRA PIECES

One of the most enjoyable aspects of owning a set of bones is finding pieces for it. Sometimes you go looking for a piece to fill a need in your set or to replace a broken piece or a piece that is just not working for you. Other times you don't know you need a certain piece until you see it. Sometimes the bones are a handy excuse to buy beautiful little items "just in case!"

Pieces need not be expensive to acquire. You can find most of the things you need for free. For example:

• **Your Home:** You may find things in your home that you have been holding onto for a long time even though you had no practical use for them, which end up being perfect for your bone set. Maybe you knew that they would be needed someday but you didn't know why. Perhaps spirit was leading you to keep them for your bone set.

• **Your Jewelry Box:** You probably have some broken pieces that could be re-purposed. Thrift shops also have inexpensive jewelry that can be broken down and used as curios.

• **Junk Drawers:** Most people have one or more boxes or drawers in which they store odds and ends. These often contain a wealth of small, meaningful items.

• **Nature:** The natural world is full of possible additions to your set. A walk in the park or even in an urban area can provide seed pods, interesting stones, twigs, snail shells (make sure they are sturdy as they sometimes have very thin and fragile spots), and even small animal bones.

• **Bead Shops and Craft Stores:** Those that have jewelry supplies have a wealth of small pendants, beads, and trinkets that are suitable for use in your bone set. Some stores have a large selection of beads carved from animal bones. These are relatively inexpensive — often less expensive than purchasing whole animal bones. Round beads are not recommended, as they are likely to roll further than you would like during casting.

- **Occult Shops:** Many vendors of starter sets for bone reading also sell single bones of various types and you can order these as "expansions" to your starter set at any time. Many of them also carry a wide selection of small amulets, talismans, and other natural pieces made of bone, stone, or wood.
- **Bone Shops:** There are several online sources of bones and many larger cities have specialty shops that carry a good selection of small and large animal bones. Between those shops, your home, and nature, you should have little trouble putting together a set of bones with pieces to cover all of the areas that you want to address in your readings.

Several sources for bone sets and individual bones are listed at the end of this book. Most maintain online stores, and several keep a presence on eBay or Etsy as well. If you are looking for a particular bone and don't see what you want, take a moment to call. Most shops have a much larger inventory than they can show on a website and their inventories change frequently.

GETTING YOUR NEW BONES READY FOR USE

When you get your new set of bones or when you add new bones to an existing set, a little preparatory work will remove any unwanted energy and make your set ready to receive your energy. This would also be a good time to look the pieces over and to start thinking about interpretive meanings for the pieces that you have gathered.

Some pieces will give their meanings to you right away while others may take some research or require you to spend some time with them before they offer their meanings. Some books suggest meanings and later in this book I supply some as well.

Some readers prefer not to alter the energy, believing that the original energy of the animal or plant is best left undisturbed. Neither way is right — proceed as you feel guided by spirit.

CLEANSING NEW BONES AND PIECES

There are several methods you can use to cleanse your bones, depending on your own approach to spiritual work. I view my bones as an intimate, spiritual tool so my first goal is to remove the energy of other people who have handled them before they got to me. Cleansing can be as simple or as elaborate as you desire. A simple method is provided here. Feel free to adapt it or change it to suit your own sensibilities.

1. Get your materials together.
- **Water:** You can do this at the sink or, if you prefer not to use tap water, you can use spring water or even holy water. A small bowl should be enough.
- **Cloth Towel or Paper Towel:** You should have enough space to lay all of the pieces out on the surface of the towel with space in between each piece to allow air to circulate.
- **Florida Water, Kananga Water, Hoyt's Cologne:** Any other scented water, whiskey, or spirits will work as well.
- **Incense:** If you want to cleanse your bone set with incense, get your materials together for burning that as well. You can burn herbs directly on charcoal or mix them with a self-lighting incense that is compatible with spiritual work.

2. Rinse each piece in the water.
You should swish it around to remove any loose dirt, rubbing soiled areas gently with your fingers, but it is not necessary to soak or scrub the pieces. Some items should not be allowed to stay wet or sit in water for any length of time as they may be damaged. Look each piece over carefully to determine if it should be allowed to get wet. Keep in mind that the goal is not to have spotless pieces. In fact some discoloring due to age or wear may be desirable because it enhances the look of your set.

3. Lay the pieces out on the towel and let them dry.

4. Swab each piece with the alcohol-based scent.
A small piece of cloth, a paper towel, a cotton pad or ball, or even a cotton swab will work well for this purpose. The goal is to swipe the entire surface of the items, but not to get them too wet or soak them. Again, care is needed to make sure the pieces you swab are alcohol safe. If you have any doubts, don't use alcohol on the piece.

5. Set the pieces aside and let them dry completely.

6. If you choose, you may smoke the bones with incense.
The incense you choose should be cleansing and attractive to spirits. A good combination to burn on charcoal is:
  • **Copal**
  • **Acacia Leaves**
  • **Benzoin**
  • **Althæa Leaves**
  • **Frankincense**
Just use a pinch of each ingredient or mix up a larger batch to have ready each time you cleanse your bones. Alternatively, add one or more of these ingredients to self-lighting incense of a suitable type for spiritual work. This recipe can easily be adapted to suit your own tastes and sensibilities.

Cleansing is a good time to reinforce the meaning of the pieces in your mind. Say the meaning as you rinse each piece, say it again as you cleanse it, or as you put each piece into the container. Do this for all of the pieces you have determined the meanings for and you will probably have them fully memorized by the time you are finished. Don't fret if you haven't come up with a meaning for every single piece yet. You can just do this for the pieces that are clear to you from the start.

Any specific cloths or storage containers that you plan to use should be cleansed as well. This is the time to thank the animals for their sacrifice and ask them if they are willing to work with you.

Hold each bone in your hand, say a prayer, wish that the animal is at peace, and ask it if it will work with you and your ancestors to help others. Sit silently holding the bone and see if you get any indication of its willingness to work with you. It could be an inner feeling or a feeling in your hand. If you get no feeling it is probably all right to use the piece. Bones with a negative feeling should be replaced immediately. You may address plant pieces in the same way, as helpful spirit allies. For inanimate objects, holding them in your hand quietly and praying that they assist you in helping yourself and others will allow those pieces to absorb your energy.

Your set is now ready to work with.

INTRODUCING BONES TO THE ANCESTORS

In cultures with a long history of bone reading the established meanings of pieces are well known to both diviners and their clients. While there may have been diviners far back in my family tree, no one in recent generations has done bone reading to my knowledge, thus my ancestors and I do not have a common language of divinatory meanings. To ensure that we understand each other I show each piece to my ancestors at my ancestor altar and explain to them what the piece means.

PIECE MEANINGS

I have about 90 pieces in my main bone set. Over time, through trial and error, I found the pieces needed to cover the areas people ask about. At one time I had more than 100 pieces, but on review, I found some piece meanings were very similar. For redundant pieces I decided which one to keep and removed the other.

My set seems to have settled down and doesn't vary much from this number. Though I seem to be always on the lookout for potential pieces, very few actually make it into my set — usually to replace a piece that breaks or stops working.

I also have a smaller set to take with me when I travel that does not necessitate careful packaging and handling. It has fewer pieces and smaller shells, allowing it to fit in a small bag or box. I use a thin suede cloth that folds up small with it as well. It is the set you see in the illustrations in this book. Here are the pieces that I have in my travel set. You can use it as a jumping off point for ideas for your own set.

BONES AND PIECES MADE OF BONE

1. Raccoon Baculum: Fidelity, loyalty, a good person who will respect and take care of you.

2. Possum Rib with a Healed Fracture: Something that was broken or has been hurt that has now healed.

3. Hamsa Hand #1: Spiritual protection if the eye side is showing, a need to seek spiritual help if palm side up.

4. Arrow: Things moving quickly or happening far away home.

5. Mink Jaws (2): One, for good speech, is left plain. One, for bad speech, is marked with three dots. Both have plain black marks on the back to distinguish whether they are speaking or silent in the reading.

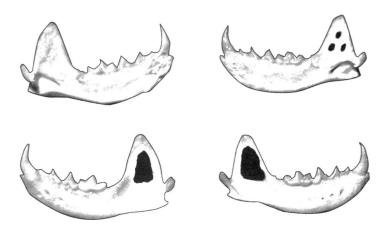

6. Coyote Baculum: Possible betrayal, trickster energy, surviving by one's wits.

7. Cougar Bone: Solitary person, stealthy, graceful, powerful.

8. Snake Rib: Constriction, being held in place.

9. Dog Bone: A faithful companion, loyalty, protection.

10. Snake Vertebra: Backbone, strength, flexibility, standing tall.

11. Lion Bone: Courage, majesty, power, pride.

12. Mask: Secrets, hidden knowledge or information.

13. Crucifix: Face up, sacrifice; face down, blessings.

14. **Die:** Gives the overall atmosphere of the reading as indicated by the number showing. I use the following number meanings, but if you are conversant with numerology or some other number interpretation system you can use it, or a variation of it, as well.
    - **1 – Beginnings.**
    - **2 – Choices.**
    - **3 – Things flowing smoothly.**
    - **4 – Stability.**
    - **5 – Strife and conflict.**
    - **6 – Things coming to an apogee.**
15. **Child:** Play or a need for play and relaxation.
16. **Goddess Figurine:** If face up, a need for ritual; if face down, silent.
17. **Hamsa Hand #2:** Palm side up, something will be received; palm down, something will be given up.
18. **Skull and Crossbones:** Fear.
19. **Skull:** Ancestors, spirits.
20. **Relationship Figures (2):** People in a relationship.
21. **Button:** Connecting.
22. **Domino:** Numbers up, the client is aware; blank side up, the client is unaware or in denial.
23. **Ethiopian Eye Pendant:** Spiritual energy, positive or negative depending on which side presents.
24. **Turtle:** Things moving slowly or not at all.

SHELLS

25. Arabic Cowrie Shell: Home.

26. Mole Cowrie Shell: Ancient ancestors.

27. Small Purple Top Cowrie Shell: Child or young person.

28. Snake Head Cowrie Shell: A young adult.

29. Money Cowrie Shell: A middle-aged or older adult.

30. Top Shell: An elderly adult.

31. Tiny Conch Shell: An unborn baby. This piece can indicate a literal pregnancy if supported by surrounding pieces, but it can also indicate something that is in the planning stages, but not yet manifest.

32. Bubble Shell: Mother and the maternal line of the family.

33. Olive Shell: Father and the paternal line of the family.

34. Rainbow Shell: Now, in the present time.

35. Mother of Pearl Bird: A message from spirit.

36. Abalone Disk: Full Moon.

37. Abalone Shell: The gifts and talents the client brings to the situation.

38. Cat's Eye Shell: If the eye side is up, seeing things clearly; if the eye side is down, the client may be in the dark or refusing to see.

39. Sea Urchin Spines (2): Separators, dividers, pointers.

STONES

40. Lapis Lazuli: Water.

41. Carnelian: Fire.

42. Citrine: Air.

43. Green Aventurine: Earth.

44. Unidentified Rough Stone: Obstacles. If standing upright, a major obstacle or obstacles that will be difficult to overcome; if laying on its side, a smaller obstacle or obstacles that can be more easily overcome.

45. Coprolite: Old issues or behaviors that no longer serve. These could be issues from the client's past. Often, but not always, they cause the client to respond in ways that are no longer appropriate or useful.

46. White Howlite: History, stories.

47. Lingam Stone: Balance.

48. Garnet Stretch Bracelet: Action. If a piece falls within the bracelet, it represents an action to be taken by the client.

METAL

49. Coins: A Penny, a Golden Cowrie Coin, and a Sacagawea Dollar Coin represent, respectively, a small, medium, and large sum of money.

50. Head: Thoughts.

51. Copper Nugget: Healing in progress.

52. Handcuffs: Being attached to something, often in an unhealthy way.

53. Woman: Gratitude.

54. Silver Cowrie Shell: A good friend.

55. Elephant: Pushing through obstacles.

56. Woman Giving Birth: Creativity.

57. Heart Milagro: Love, emotions, the heart.

58. Key: Opportunities, doors opening or closing.

59. Fishing Weight: Carrying a heavy burden or load.

60. Tiger Bell: I have marked my Tiger Bell with eyes "open" on one side and "closed" on the other side. If eyes open, a warning; if closed, silent.

61. Ring: Relationships, love, commitment.

62. Crescent Moon: New Moon; activities taking place but not seen.

63. Yin Yang Bead: Good fortune if Yin Yang symbol shows, silent if not.

64. Thimble: Work, employment.

CERAMICS AND GLASS

65. Raku Figurine: The client.

66. Dollhouse Bowl: If open side up, need; if bottom side up, silent.

67. Clear Gem, Diamond, or Rhinestone: Pay attention.

68. Frog: Transformation.

69. Shoe: Travel.

70. Doll Head: Spirit guide.

71. Doll Arm: Help or assistance.

72. Mirror: Looking inward, introspection.

SEEDS, PODS, HERBS

73. Buckeye Nut: Health. Stem or "eye" side up indicates a health issue, smooth side up indicates good health.
74. Little John to Chew Root: Law, rules, legal issues.
75. John the Conqueror Root: Masculine energy, force, confidence.
76. Nutmeg: Luck.
77. Queen Elizabeth Root: Feminine energy, allure, nurture.
78. Master Root: Mastery, accomplishment, achievement.

Once you have assigned meanings to all of the pieces in your set and shown them to your ancestors, this is not to say that the meanings are carved in stone and that you can never deviate from what you have shown them. For instance, a piece that is normally seen in a negative light, could, under certain circumstances, be seen in a positive light.

If, when doing a reading, you see a piece that has a certain meaning and you get a strong feeling that it means something else this time, go with that feeling.

I find when this happens and I explain to the client that "This piece normally means A, but I am getting a strong feeling that this time it means B," more often than not they will pipe in with an explanation. Even when they don't, I sometimes find that they will tell me later, "Remember that piece that didn't make sense to you in the reading? Here is what happened."

A good list of possible meanings for the bones of various animals and types of bones can be found in the book *Throwing the Bones* by catherine yronwode.

MARKING PIECES

You may notice that some pieces have more than one meaning depending on how they present, or on which side they fall. Some pieces naturally have a clearly distinguishable top and bottom. Other pieces may have different aspects, but they may be too subtle to identify quickly. I mark these pieces to make identification easier. An example is my Mink Jaw bones. If you look at them they do have two different sides – at the side furthest from the teeth, one side is convex and one side is concave. However, you have to look carefully to see which side is which. I made them easier to see by marking one side with a black mark. If the black mark is showing, the piece is silent. I also have two Mink Jaws. One is for positive speech and the other for negative speech. I put three small dots on the jaw for negative speech.

THE VERSATILITY OF SHELLS

Shells are extremely versatile in a bone set. They come in many sizes, shapes, and colors that are easily distinguishable from one another when reading. I use shells primarily to represent people — old, young, male, and female. But they can be used to represent anything you want. I use the Rainbow Shell to represent "now," and I use Sea Urchin Spines as dividers and pointers.

Shells can also be used on an as-needed basis to add detail to a reading. For example if someone comes to you with a reading about a situation involving their boss, you can grab a shell and assign it to be their boss in the throw.

When I first started reading for others I was experimenting with different methods of casting. I used to give the client a Sand Dollar to represent him or herself and have the client throw it into the spread after I made my casting. As I started doing more distance readings, this became impractical.

Clients usually appreciate getting a tangible reminder of their reading that they can carry with them or put on their altar as a reminder or affirmation. Sand Dollars are pretty, plentiful, and inexpensive. Usually I would let them keep the Sand Dollar at the end of the reading.

When purchasing shells, other than cowrie shells for throwing, look them over carefully, especially the edges. Try to avoid those with thin edges as they can chip easily or break.

EXTRA PIECES

Some readers have pieces for specific situations that they do not always maintain in their sets. I used to do this with my "couple in a relationship" pieces. I would only add them if the question was about a relationship. Over time I found it easier to just leave them in the set.

I still carry extra pieces for readings where there are several people involved. I give them to clients and show them — this is person A, this is person B, this is person C, etc. I have them hold each piece in their hands while they think about the people. This works well and makes the clients more active participants in their readings. You will be surprised how attentive they become asking questions about the pieces representative of each party involved.

I have also found these pieces useful for readings where the presented issue was not about a relationship, as they sometimes show how the stated issue is impacting the relationship, or they may highlight an issue with the relationship that the client should be made aware of.

HOW MANY PIECES?

Starting out, you want to keep the number of pieces you are working with rather small to avoid feeling overwhelmed, while still having enough pieces to cover the situations you are likely to be asked to about.

I have found that there are certain topics that frequently come up in readings. You can assign these topic-meanings to pieces already in your set, but if you add new pieces to represent these topics, don't forget to go through the same steps of cleansing and introduction that you did for your original pieces.

- **A piece to represent yourself or the client:** I have found that having a piece specifically for this purpose gives me a focal point or starting point for the reading. I use a small raku figure for this. The piece does not have to be a figure. It can be anything at all — a sea shell, a curio, or even a human bone. Your Client Piece may have an up-side and a down-side. This can provide additional insight into the client's state of mind.
- **A piece to represent financial issues:** Coins are an obvious choice, but I have also used a carved peach pit with the Chinese symbol for good fortune. Money and finances touch almost every area of our lives and people whose issues seem to have nothing to do with money on the surface often end up asking about the financial aspects of it before the reading is over.
- **Two pieces to represent a couple:** These can be any two things that are distinguishable from one another. I use two pieces of sea shell, one short and light, the other long and dark. Readers who do a lot of relationship readings may have additional pieces for different kinds of relationships, but the two pieces for a couple are a good beginning.
- **A piece to represent "now":** This helps to gauge when things are taking place. Things closer to this piece are current and things farther out are less current.

- **A piece to represent home:** This piece can shed further light on domestic issues. Many of the situations we are concerned about happen in or around the home.
- **An "action" piece:** I use a Garnet Bracelet for this. Things falling within the Bracelet are actions to be undertaken by the client. It is rare that nothing falls inside the Bracelet.

A TRAVEL SET

My travel set is smaller than my home set, having around 70 pieces. To limit the number of pieces, I have eliminated some significators of in-depth or deep situations and conditions. For instance, my main set has pieces to represent male and female ancestors from several generations in both the maternal and paternal line, while my travel set includes only parents and one generalized "ancestor" piece.

USEFUL PIECES FOR A LARGER SET OF BONES

If your set gets large — 50 or more pieces — there are some additional pieces that may make interpretation a little easier. A large set will usually break down into several fairly discrete groupings when cast. If time is unlimited then you can interpret them all, but if you are doing readings in a limited time frame, then reading every group may not be possible. In those cases, having a few helper pieces may be valuable.

- **Dividers:** I use Sea Urchin Spines as dividers. They can also be used as pointers. My main set has four and my travel set two. They help to show distinctions between groups. They can also point to important groups or pieces. Sometimes they can indicate a path in the reading, or an obstacle, and how to overcome it. You can use anything that is fairly thin and long such as quartz crystals or even twigs.

- **Diamond:** I use a Herkimer Diamond in my main set and a Glass Rhinestone in my travel set to say "look over here!" These bright pieces catch and reflect the light in such a way as to draw your attention to them if they are not completely covered by another piece. I interpret whatever group they are in, regardless of where it is located in relation to the client and the now pieces, because I read the Diamond as indicating something the client needs to know.

- **People:** I have many people-pieces in my set, which is one reason that my set is so large. My travel set has fewer people — only one ungendered piece to represent a child, a young adult, an older adult, a middle aged person, and an unborn baby, which can mean a literal pregnancy or an idea that is germinating, but has not yet come to fruition. In my main set, I have two differently-sized shells of the same species to represent the Male Piece and Female Piece for each age group, except for the unborn baby – almost doubling the number of people-pieces. I also have more pieces to represent the ancestors and other spirits in my home set than in my travel set.

As you start to do readings you will sometimes find yourself wishing that you had a piece to shed more light on a situation. That is one way that extra pieces get added over time. Or you could establish your set with extra pieces from the beginning to represent areas you work with.

One reader I know who is also an astrologer has added pieces for the planets to her set. Another reader, who works with relationships a lot in his practice, has several pieces that address different relationship issues.

If you think you will find it useful to have pieces to address something specific, add them and see how they work for you. If you find that they don't contribute anything to your readings, you can always remove them.

CREATING A BONE JOURNAL

Once you have the pieces you think you will need, you may want to write them down in a notebook or on index cards. You can photograph the set and cut out individual pieces to paste into a journal, sketch them in, or make an unillustrated list.

Unlike tarot and other divination systems that require you to learn a baseline of traditional meanings, contemporary bone reading is more intuitive. That can be both a blessing and a curse. Once mastered, structured systems give you a solid framework from which to work. Self-defined systems can feel a little wobbly at first, by comparison, but once you have decided what each piece means, you will probably find that your set fits you like a glove.

Coming from a tarot background, I brought much of that structure to my bone reading. I had an abbreviated spread outlined on my cloth or in my mind and I limited the number of pieces I read by reaching in and grabbing just a handful. My readings using this sortilege method provided good information, but by forcing the reading into this framework my intellect was in the forefront. My mind was busy categorizing and organizing when the ancestors and spirit were trying to speak to me. Once I got over my fear and let go of that familiar framework, I found that my readings began to flow.

If you feel more comfortable with a framework and a system, by all means use it. It is certainly helpful when starting out to gain confidence in your ability to divine with this method. Your readings will still yield good information, and after all, that is what we are here for. But I think you will find that getting your thinking mind out of the way will open you to even more information. Try it. If you find that you are drawing a blank, feeling overwhelmed, or just not ready, just go back to a more structured approach and try again in the future. Over time, as your relationship with the bones, the ancestors, and spirit grows you may find it easier to let go and trust the guidance you are receiving from spirit.

ACCOUTREMENTS

There are some items that I like to have with me whenever I am going to do a reading. They are not required items – all you really need is a set of bones and a surface to read them on. But I have found them useful to have on hand to set the mood or to help with readings on unusual subjects.

- **Hoyt's Cologne:** I use Hoyt's Cologne to cleanse and cool my bones after every reading. I do this by putting a little on my fingers and then running them through the bones.
- **Extra Shells:** I like to have a few extra shells of various sizes, shapes, and colors with me to represent things or people that I don't have a piece to represent. If I get a question about a relationship between two people, I have a couple in my set already. But if I get a question about three or more people I can just choose shells to represent additional people.
- **Porcupine Quill:** I use the porcupine quill to manipulate bones on the throwing surface if necessary during a reading. This is most often needed when one of more pieces cover another one. Alternatively, you could use a feather, stick, or pointer. You can even use your hands for the task, but many readers prefer not to touch the bones during a reading.
- **Rattle and Bells:** I use a gourd rattle and bells to call the ancestors. By shaking the rattle and ringing the bells I find it easier to shift into the proper state of mind for the reading. I also think the spirits respond quicker to the sound than they do to just a regularly spoken invocation.
- **Candles and Candlestick:** I like to have fire near the reading surface. I light a candle for every reading and place it on my altar to finish burning when the reading is complete. White household candles or tea lights are perfect for this. A wood or brass candlestick travels well and is not likely to break when I am on the road.

- **Ceramic or Glass Bowl of Water:** I like to have water near the reading surface.
- **Anointing Oil:** Carrying a small bottle of dressing oil can be useful. When the client has a goal, giving them a simple Crown of Success head anointing at the end of the reading can do wonders for their self-confidence.

I keep some of these items in a small pouch when traveling. Again, this list is not mandatory and you are free to add to or adapt it to your particular style and sensibilities.

READING SURFACE

You will have to decide what to use for a reading surface. A piece of cloth, a straw mat, or a small rug would all work well. You may want to keep any pattern or decoration simple so that it will not be distracting.

I use a piece of suede cowhide layered over a piece of fabric. The fabric is sewn onto a quilted backing for extra cushioning. The extra cushioning is important when I am throwing onto hard surfaces because my set has a lot of sea shells. The skin is plain black so as not to be distracting.

As your set grows, you may find that your reading surface gets too small. Conversely, you don't want a huge throwing surface for a set that consists of only a few small pieces. I find that I enjoy reading more if my reading surface is aesthetically pleasing.

When I first started reading, I used a cloth with a set of crossed lines on it. I read the pieces in the upper half of the cross as things that are happening on a conscious level or in the material world and pieces in the bottom half as things that are happening on an unconscious level or in the world of the spirits. Things on the left were passing away and things on the right were coming into being.

Those familiar with card-based forms of divination may recognize this system from spreads they have used. This system worked well for me and gave me a structure that reduced my uncertainty in interpreting. Alternatively, use this method with a plain surface by imagining the cross on it and reading accordingly. Of course you can use any other system that you feel comfortable with – the four seasons, the elements, the houses or signs of the zodiac, the compass directions; whatever feels right to you.

After studying with an experienced reader and practicing many hours I gained enough confidence to dispense with this structured method and allow myself to be guided by spirit. Try a structured method for yourself and see if you find it helpful.

The Reading Cloth of Bonemaster Ka

THROWING TECHNIQUES

You will have to decide how you want to throw your bones. The easiest way if you don't have too many pieces, is to simply throw them from your hands. You can also throw them from a container such as a basket or a small box. If you are reading for a client, you can even have the client throw them. An alternative is to have the client throw particular bones, such as the Client Piece, the Relationship Pieces, or a giveaway piece like the Sand Dollar.

You should practice your throwing technique so that it is smooth and effortless. With practice you will determine how hard or gently to toss them out or how high to drop them in order to get a good distribution of pieces. You don't want to drop them so that they fall into a single heap, nor do you want them to spread out so far that they start falling outside the designated reading surface with no pieces in proximity to each other.

LET'S THROW THE BONES!

You have your bone set with all the pieces you want to start out with. You have cleansed them and introduced them to your ancestors. You've tossed them a few times to get a feel for how to throw them. Now you are ready to do a practice reading.

I find it helpful to set a mood for my reading. I might light some incense, have a candle and some flowers nearby, and a glass or bowl of water at hand. While many traditional readers work on the ground or the floor, I have also seen readers use their living room coffee table or kitchen table. Whatever you decide, make an effort to make the area attractive and as distraction-free as possible.

Before I begin a reading I pray and ask deity to assist me. I also call on my ancestors and if I am reading for someone else I call in their ancestors as well. I ask for their assistance and help in giving the client the best advice possible.

I have a string of bells that I wrap around my hand and shake and I use a rattle in the other hand as I call the ancestors. I believe they recognize the sounds, and it also helps me shift consciousness quickly. One of my teachers sings her invocations. This sets a wonderful tone and mood for the reading.

I usually ask the client what the reading will be about. If the issue can benefit from adding pieces to the set or by designating pieces to represent various people involved I do so at this time. I then ask the client to breathe on the bones three times while thinking about their question.

If it is a distance reading via telephone or Skype I breathe the client's question into the bones.

GETTING A FEEL FOR THE READING

Once you have thrown the bones, take a few moments to get a feel for the reading. Look it over before you speak. At first glance the throw can look like a confusing, meaningless jumble.

This is where having a focal piece to represent yourself or the client comes in. Look for that piece. What pieces are close to it? Where are those pieces in relation to the Client Piece's body? Are they near the head? That could be what is on the clients mind, even if they have not said so. Is the Client Piece "standing" on a piece? Perhaps this is an area that is foundational to the client. Or the client could be restraining something by stepping on it or even stepping on it with malice. Pieces around the Client Piece will usually be very important.

Are there several distinct groups of pieces? After you have interpreted the pieces closest to the client you can start reading the groups of pieces nearby and work your way out from there.

Next you can look for the piece that represents "Now." What is happening around that piece? The pieces there will give you an idea of what is going on in the client's life at present.

Are pieces piled up on top of each other or chaotic in their appearance? Do they present an easily distinguishable path for the client to follow? Are there many pieces around the Head, suggesting worry? These things are suggestive of what is going on with the client.

Does your eye and attention go to a certain area right away? Perhaps that is where the reading should begin.

Looking for these types of things before you open your mouth to speak will help you get a feel for the reading. Don't be afraid to take a deep breath and look at the throw to get your bearing. A few moments of silence will not detract from the reading and will show your client that you are a thoughtful reader.

Once you start speaking you can describe what you see near the Client Piece first. Then you can move on to the "Now" piece, or on to other groupings and describe what you see there.

I interpret pieces as being weaker the further they are from the Client Piece and/or Rainbow Shell that represents "Now." Sometimes the Client Piece is isolated and far from the other pieces. This can be interpreted as the client being detached from what is going on, or being unwilling to get involved.

INTERPRETING THE THROW

In teaching classes I have found that many people have the same problem I did. They know what the individual bones mean but have difficulty making sense of them in groups. Or they try to read the whole throw at once rather than breaking it down into its component parts.

Some throws result in groups where the bones are piled up in a heap, with pieces at the bottom less visible or even totally hidden. You will have to determine how you want to handle this when it occurs. Some readers just read the visible piece on the top, while others will gently separate the pieces to reveal the underlying bones and interpret them with the group as well.

At the other end of the spectrum is the throw that results in most of the pieces being far away from each other. Here it is useful to look for a pattern or a path that can be followed as you weave your interpretation.

Time spent practicing your throwing technique will minimize both of these types of throws, though it is unlikely that you will never have to deal with them. Don't let this type of throw cause you to feel stress. Take your time, look the pieces over, ask for guidance from spirit, and read the throw.

POSSIBLE PROBLEMS

Sometimes pieces break. You should think about what you are going to do when that happens. You will probably find that you grow attached to your bones and will grieve a little for a broken piece. Disposal should be done in a manner befitting a sacred tool. You can thank the piece for its service and bury it or dispose of it in nature.

However, you don't have to dispose of a piece because it breaks. You can decide to keep on using it as-is or give it a new meaning. One reader I know had a piece that represented the client. At some point it broke into two pieces with the head separating from the body. Rather than discard the pieces, she decided to use it as it was. She says it lets her know where the client's mind is at. I adapted this idea in my set by adding the small metal Head for this same purpose.

Sometimes a piece may seem to stop working. It falls to the edge of the cloth most of the time, or it creates a sense of confusion to the reading rather than clarity. When this happens I remove the piece and set it aside. If it is an important piece, I either replace it or try to read without it and see how that goes. Sometimes those pieces find their way back into my set after a time. But usually if a piece stops working, I thank it for its service and set it on my altar in a small bowl.

CLOSING THE READING

Once you have finished the reading and answered any questions the client may have you should thank the ancestors, spirits and deities that you called at the beginning of the reading. If I am at home I usually show appreciation by providing a shot glass of spirits at the conclusion of my readings for the day.

PRACTICE

This is a divination method that requires practice to master. You have to practice your throwing technique, you have to practice your invocations and prayers, you have to practice interpreting the bones, and you have to practice closing the reading. Nothing deflates your client's confidence faster than the reader looking flustered and unsure during the reading.

Starting out, I would practice every chance I got. I offered (insisted on) free readings for my friends. When I exhausted them I rented a space (very cheaply) one day a week and started offering free readings locally to whoever signed up. I also offered to swap bone readings in various on-line forums with anyone who was willing. I read for myself frequently, almost daily. Once I felt comfortable, I started reading professionally.

Swapping readings with other bone readers is an excellent way to expand your skills. No two bone readers read alike and I cannot think of a single reading I swapped or paid for from another reader that did not teach me something new and useful.

Don't be afraid to swap readings because you are inexperienced. Every reader was new at some point and most remember what it felt like. Let them help you the way others helped them. You will often find that if you swap with experienced readers they will be happy to answer any questions about their technique that come up during the reading.

If you are having difficulty interpreting groups of bones, try throwing just a few pieces and interpreting what they mean. If necessary, start with two pieces. Throw them several times and describe how you would interpret them together. Sometimes beginning with a piece representing a person is best.

Using the Client Piece in your practice throws will help you to get into the habit of looking at that piece first. But don't limit yourself to using the Client Piece, because you will also have to interpret clusters of bones that are separated from the Client Piece.

As you gain confidence in interpreting small groups of bones, add more pieces until you are interpreting your entire set. Keep in mind that a throw using a big set of bones usually results in several smaller groups on the reading surface.

Even now I sometimes look at a group of bones and feel a bit challenged! But I know to go somewhere else in the reading and come back to that group. Usually the rest of the reading provides information that makes the challenging portions clearer.

CLEANSING IN BETWEEN READINGS

If you do several readings a day, you might want to devise a way to remove the previous client's energy before the next client comes in. Time usually does not allow for an elaborate cleansing ritual. I carry Hoyt's Cologne with my bones and splash a bit on my fingers and run them through the bones between readings. It has the sensation of cooling them down between readings.

When I first began reading, I would hold hands with the client while calling on deity, the client's ancestors, my ancestors, and the spirits. I would swish the bones in their container for the client after they had breathed their question into them. To clear my hands between readings I carried a small copper bowl. After a reading I would rinse my hands with water and cup the copper bowl for a few moments to let it absorb any outside energy.

I also work at events, and after a day of reading for many clients back to back, I usually do a good cleansing or at least run the bones through some cleansing incense. This is in addition to cooling the bones between each reading using Hoyt's Cologne. If you store your bones in a woven basket you can often hold the basket full of bones over the incense smoke and allow it to permeate the bones through the weave of the basket. You will probably start to notice a desire for some type of neutralizing activity between clients if you start to read in any volume. If you are doing only one reading every now and then, the energy will most likely dissipate on its own between readings. Still, a cleansing ritual of some type at the end of each reading is a good habit to get into.

HOW LONG?

A full reading with a large set can take well over an hour. This will generally entail your interpreting all of the pieces or almost every piece on the cloth. However, you can shorten that time by being selective about the groups you interpret. You can do a reading in a very short time if you concentrate on the pieces around the Client Piece and the pieces around the "Now" piece. Or you can tailor the reading: If the question is about a relationship, read the

pieces that apply to a relationship in addition to the pieces around the client. Or, if it is about work, interpret the work piece (the Thimble) and any work-related pieces in addition to what is going on around the Client Piece.

DECISION READING

I learned this from one of my teachers who is a sangoma. If you have to make a decision you can write out your choices on small sheets of paper and put them on the edges of your cloth, one to a side.

Do a throw and read the pieces closest to each choice. Those pieces speak to the outcome for that course of action.

Alternately you can do a separate throw for each choice. You will get more detailed information that way, but sometimes you can find that time is limited or that several throws can be too much of a good thing. This method allows you to see the alternatives laid out with the strengths and weaknesses of each.

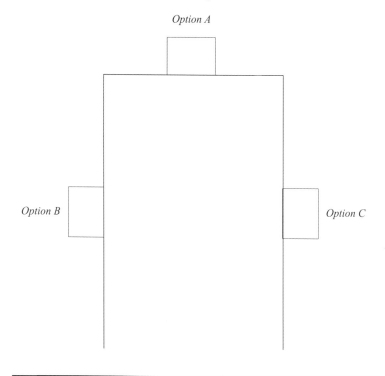

Option A

Option B

Option C

RELATIONSHIP READING

If you don't have pieces for a couple, you can add them for this reading. Choose two pieces (more if applicable), and designate the identity of each piece as you set your intention for the reading.

If the reading is in person, you can have the client hold each piece while thinking about the person it was chosen to represent. Once thrown, look to see where the pieces land and what is nearby. Are they close together? Are they on opposite sides of the cloth? Is the Ring near one, between the two, far from either of them?

I have found that when I do this with clients they pay little attention to the rest of the reading — their eyes follow the pieces for the protagonists and the pieces near them. However, the rest of the throw has valuable information about the state of the relationship as well. Don't let where the protagonist pieces fall blind you to otherwise vital information shown in the reading.

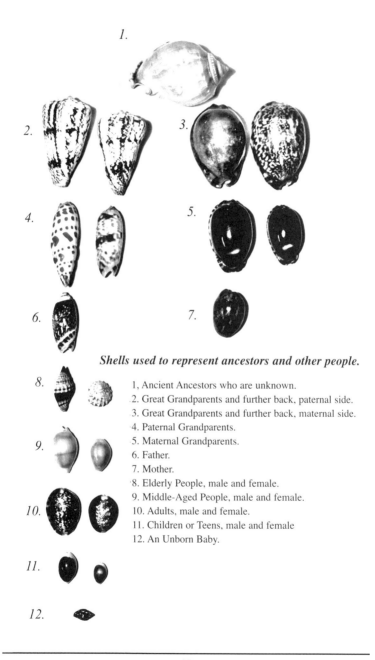

Shells used to represent ancestors and other people.

1, Ancient Ancestors who are unknown.
2. Great Grandparents and further back, paternal side.
3. Great Grandparents and further back, maternal side.
4. Paternal Grandparents.
5. Maternal Grandparents.
6. Father.
7. Mother.
8. Elderly People, male and female.
9. Middle-Aged People, male and female.
10. Adults, male and female.
11. Children or Teens, male and female
12. An Unborn Baby.

ANCESTOR READING

I have used this type of reading to converse with my ancestors with excellent results. If you don't have pieces to represent your ancestors in your bone set, you can add designated pieces just for this throw, though I keep pieces for my ancestors in my main set at all times.

First I do a throw with my intention being to have any ancestor that wished to speak to me do so. My intention is that a particular piece in my set will be the indication that the ancestor wishes to speak. I use a shell Bird for this purpose.

I do the throw and look to see where that particular piece has landed. If there is an ancestor nearby — or better still touching that piece — I read the pieces surrounding the ancestor to see what the ancestor wishes to tell me about him or herself. I also look at the rest of the reading to see if anything jumps out at me, but the point of this first throw is to gain insight on who wishes to communicate with me.

When I am finished with that first throw, I gather all of the pieces and remove any pieces that represent ancestors from the set, except for the ancestor who indicated that he or she wishes to speak. I do a second throw with just those pieces and interpret it as what more that particular ancestor wanted to say.

My travel set has a piece to represent the ancestors (a Skull), a piece to represent the maternal line (Bubble Shell), a piece to represent the paternal line (Olive Shell), and a piece to represent ancient ancestors unknown to the client (Mole Cowrie Shell). My main set has a mother, father, grandparents for the maternal and paternal lines, and pieces for ancient female and male ancestors on the maternal and paternal sides.

A sample of the shells that can be used to represent several types and generations of people is shown in the illustration. It is similar to what I have in my main set.

TALKING TO A PARTICULAR ANCESTOR

In South African sangoma bone sets there are several pieces that represent people and various ancestors. My set has similar pieces representing generations on both sides of my family.

I was sitting in my yard reading one day when I got a strong message that one of my ancestors had a message for me and that I should do a reading taking all of the other ancestors out of my set so that she could speak to me.

I asked myself "why didn't she just give me the message in a reading with the other ancestors present?," but then it occurred to me that she had tried but perhaps her unique message was being lost in the myriad of meanings each throw represents.

I did a reading as I felt led to do it – with the other ancestor pieces removed, and it was very helpful to me with an issue I had been struggling with for some time. The guidance I received was totally on point with the issue and as soon as I looked the spread over I knew just what was being addressed. The reading showed me a clear way through something that I had been avoiding for quite some time and helped me make a firm decision that I needed to make. Try this for yourself. You can do this with an ancestor that you knew in life, or one that you didn't know.

Just like you can add pieces to represent the people in a relationship, you can add pieces to represent your ancestors or any particular spirits that you work with. You can add them when you want to talk to them specifically, or you can leave them in the set all of the time as I do.

If you decide to leave these pieces in your set all of the time then they represent your ancestors when reading for yourself and the client's ancestors when reading for someone else. Most are interested in hearing what their ancestors have to say to them and a bone reading has led to several of my clients setting up an ancestor altar to re-establish a relationship with their ancestors.

READINGS FOR SPIRITUAL WORK

As a spiritual worker I do readings for clients almost daily. If someone requests spiritual work I do a reading before taking the case to determine whether the work will be successful. I also do readings to determine which type of work would be best for a particular case.

Sometimes a reading done purely for divination purposes indicates that further work would be helpful for their issue. One of the ways I determine what type of work will be most helpful is by looking for the pieces in the Bracelet (action) and near the Goddess (ritual).

I have four stones to represent earth, air, fire, and water. If the earth piece was near, I might tell them to get a charm or a mojo bag of some type. If the air piece was nearby I might tell them to meditate or pray. If the fire piece, candle work could be in order; and if the water piece, a spiritual bath might be called for. You could take this further — earth and water together, bathing and a mojo bag. Air and fire — prayer and candles. Earth and air – mojo bag and prayer. You get the idea.

You could take this a step further by having pieces that are specific to a type of working that you do or that is your specialty. You could have supplementary pieces that you add to your set only for this purpose. You could even make a smaller set with just those pieces and use it only for the purpose of deciding a course of action that is most likely to yield results.

SAMPLE READINGS

These are readings I did for clients or myself using my travel set. The pieces and their meanings were described previously, so you can follow along and see how I came up with the interpretations I provide. You may look at these throws and come up with entirely different interpretations. That is fine. Each throw can be interpreted in more than one way.

With a larger number of pieces your throw will usually give you several groups or clumps of pieces. The readings look at these groups, providing a description and interpretation of each. It is rarely necessary to read every piece in every reading. As you gain experience you will be able to quickly identify which pieces or groups are most relevant.

SAMPLE READING 1
Is My Business Jinxed?

This was a throw for a client who wanted information on his home business, specifically whether someone was working to keep him from prospering financially.

Keep in mind that the interpretations described here are just one of many ways that each group of pieces can be interpreted.

The groupings are also arbitrary here. You may look at the total spread and decide to break it up in a totally different way. Each reader is guided by their own ancestors and spirits.

Although this spread is an actual reading done for a client, the things I am describing here are not necessarily the way I interpreted the reading for the client. During the actual reading I am in a slightly altered place mentally and I try to stay open to guidance from the ancestors to the maximum extent possible. This description is more of an intellectual interpretation than a spiritual one in order to show you the mechanics of a reading.

Taking a few moments to look over the throw, I notice a few things immediately:

The Thimble, which represents one's work, is far away from the Client Piece on the upper left of the cloth. In fact. it is far away from everything. This suggests that the client is not really interested in the work or that the work is being neglected. It could also indicate that the client's real interest in getting a reading lies elsewhere. Sometimes clients ask something neutral or less important on the first throw to see how it goes before asking their real question.

The Die shows the number two which, for me, indicates that the reading is about a choice or choices.

Let's start with the section containing the Client.

The Client Piece is touched by the Doll Arm (help or assistance) and the Snake Vertebra (strength, backbone, flexibility). This could indicate that the client has received help (Doll Arm) and has had to be strong and flexible in the face of adversity (Snake Vertebra). That these pieces are behind the Client could indicate that this influence is passing away. If they were further away from the Client Piece I would probably read them that way, but the fact that they are touching the Client and even appear to be supporting the Client could indicate that this is happening now.

The Elephant (knocking down obstacles) is near the Head. It is touching the Hamsa Hand: #2 (palm up — receiving something) and the Doll Head (a spirit helper or guardian angel). This could indicate that the client is considering getting spiritual help for their problems or obstacles with their business. This is supported by the fact that they are getting a reading and may seek additional spiritual help.

The Tiger Bell is near the Elephant as well, with the eyes showing which indicates a warning. This is all sitting on the Full Moon piece which can indicate an actual time (the next Full Moon) or Full Moon energy – things coming to the apogee.

There is a Money Cowrie nearby. This represents an older or middle aged adult – late 30s to early 60s in age. This could be the client's business partner.

Finally the Frog (transformation) is in this group, but it is silent because it is lying on its back. This could be interpreted as telling us that things are not going to change substantially.

Next we have this small group. The Carnelian (fire) is at the top touching the Coprolite (old ways of thinking and acting that may no longer serve us).

The Skull is nearby (a spirit or ancestor). These three pieces could indicate some type of dysfunction in the past or that family history is exerting a powerful effect on this issue. Perhaps some issue from the past is affecting the way the client is approaching or running his business. It could be lack of confidence or fear of failure or looking bad that is making the client afraid to expand or just the opposite – being reckless due to overconfidence.

There is not much information here other than what was just stated. Conversation with the client could reveal more if the client felt comfortable discussing it further.

This group is near the client's feet. The Mink Jaw (speech, both positive or negative) is overlaying the Skull and Crossbones (fear). The jaw is showing the inactive side, indicated by the mark on it. This could indicate the client

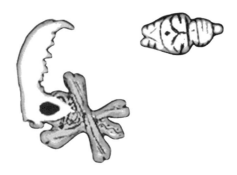

has some fears that he or she is not speaking of. That this group is under the client's feet could indicate that the client is stepping on the fear – holding it down and not expressing it.

The small Goddess Piece (ritual) is face up indicating that some type of ritual or spiritual work could be helpful.

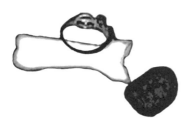

Here we have the Lion Bone (courage, pride, and power) with the Ring (relationships) laying across it. Nearby is the Lapis Lazuli stone (water). This could be interpreted as a high degree of emotional investment in the business, possibly related to feelings of pride and power. The business and its success may also be critical to important relationships in the client's life.

This next small group has the other Mink Jaw also face down indicating that it is inactive or indicating silence. The John the Conqueror Root (power, force, male energy, strength, success) is on top and the Little John Root (law, rules, doing things by the book) is beneath.

These two pieces together could be interpreted as a need to run the business "by the book," keeping accurate records, and filing documents in a timely manner in order to be successful. This could also be interpreted as following the rules being one of the business' strengths.

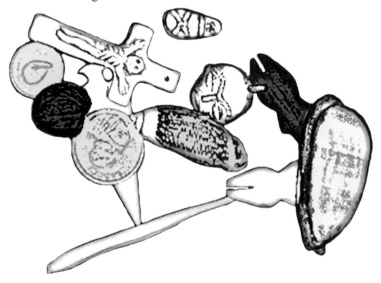

This group is fairly close to the Client Piece making it important. We have the Mole Cowrie (ancient ancestors or spirits) on the far right, the Couple Pieces (people involved in a relationship) – one face up and one face down and both under the ancestor piece. This could be interpreted as the partners in the business are being watched over by their ancestors. Both partners have strong spiritual protection.

One of the partners, the dark one, is face down, indicating that they may be less interested or involved in what is going on with the business. He or she may have started pulling away. The Head (thoughts) is touching this piece, indicating that they may be thinking less about the business or they may be distracted by something else.

The Olive Shell (paternal line) is touching the Head – perhaps the distracted partner is thinking about a family member on their paternal side.

The other partner, the light one, is face up, indicating active involvement. There may be some imbalance here between the partners. Certainly we see a difference in the amount of engagement with one partner face up, active, and possibly worried, while the other partner seems distracted and preoccupied.

The Coyote Baculum (trickster, possible betrayal, surviving by one's wits) is also touching this partner. There could be some betrayal around this partner or they could be surviving by their wits or at least feeling like they are. When this piece lands convex side up I read it as much stronger. On its side like this it is more a possibility than a sure thing. I would warn the client to be careful in his or her dealings to avoid being tricked or betrayed.

The Shoe (travel) on top could indicate a trip or travel.

The Crucifix (sacrifice or blessings) is face up, indicating sacrifice. It is on top of the Arrow (things moving quickly or far from home). The Sacagawea Dollar Coin (a large sum of money) is on top of the Arrow. The Nutmeg (luck) is on top of the Dollar Coin and it is on top of the Golden Cowrie Coin (a medium amount of money – not insignificant, but not a huge sum).

This grouping could be interpreted several ways depending on what the client has told you. Travel is possible that will require some financial sacrifice to make. With luck the cost could come down to a more manageable amount. The travel could take the client far from home.

On the other hand it may not be about travel at all. However some type of sacrifice is looming involving finances. Luck could ameliorate the cost. Things could move quickly and the client should be careful to avoid being ripped off.

I would engage in a dialogue with the client for this portion to determine the most likely meaning and I would point out alternative interpretations as well.

This group has the Hamsa Hand #1 (spiritual help and protection) eye-side up (spiritual protection), the Mask (secrets) face down indicating it is silent, a Sea Urchin Spine (divider or pointer) inside the Garnet Bracelet (actions to be taken), the Snake Rib (constriction) also inside the Garnet Bracelet.

The White Stone (history or stories) is touching the Snake Rib, the Woman (gratitude) is also touching the rib, but it is face down.

The Arabic Cowrie (home) is on top of the Woman and the Heart (love, affection) face down or inactive. The Heart is barely visible peeking out from the upper edge of the shell.

The Turtle (things moving slowly) is also touching the Garnet Bracelet though it is not inside it. It is on its back indicating that it is inactive or it could indicate that the client feels like he is not getting anywhere despite struggling like a turtle on its back.

This group indicates that the client has good spiritual protection (Hamsa Hand #1, eye side up). Nothing important is hidden from the client (Mask, facedown). The Snake Rib (constriction) inside the Bracelet (action) advises caution or circumspection.

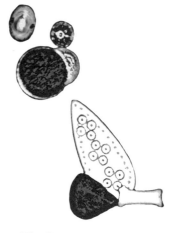

This group has the Silver Cowrie at the top left (a good friend) face down, indicating inaction. Below this, the Penny (small amount of money) is under the Mirror (looking within). The Diamond (pay heed) is to the right, touching the Penny.

The Protection Pendant (spiritual energy) is face down, indicating negative energy around the client. On top of this is the Green Aventurine (earth) and the Cougar Bone (independence).

The Penny and Mirror could speak of being aware of frittering away money on oneself to feel good – retail therapy. The spending could be due to loneliness (friend piece is face down), or just self-indulgence. The Diamond says this is important to the issue.

The Protection Pendant indicates negative energy but the pieces sitting on it point to an answer involving something concrete (earth) that the client could do for him or herself (Cougar Bone),

Earth in this regard could indicate a mojo bag, lodestone or some other spiritual work that can be attributed to the earth.

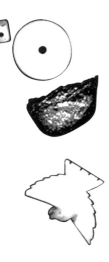

With the exception of the Die, the distance of these pieces from the Client makes them less important to the reading. The Die shows number two which I interpret as a choice or choices. The Button (connection), the Unidentified Rough Stone (small obstacles, as it is laying on its side) and the Bird (a message from spirit) all seem rather disconnected from each other, and the Bird is lying face down, indicating inaction.

This group has the Rainbow Shell ("Now") left of the face up Domino (the client is aware; if face down, the client would have been unaware). The Abalone Shell (the client's helpful talents) is to the right of the Domino. The Citrine (air) is to its right, and the Raccoon Baculum (faithfulness, loyalty, being cared for and supported) is also nearby. The Bowl (need, as it is face-up) and the Yin Yang bead (good fortune) sit on the left.

At lower right the Woman Giving Birth Pendant (creativity) is touching the Dog Bone (a loyal companion, protection), which is touching the Key (a door opening or closing). The Copper Nugget (healing) is on the far right. This group is rather far from the client, diminishing its importance, but it contains the "Now" piece.

The Bowl (need) and Yin Yang (good fortune) indicate a need for luck. The pieces closest to the Abalone Shell seem to say that the client's intellect (Citrine, air), faithfulness (Raccoon Baculum), and awareness (Domino) are skills that could be applied to good effect in this situation. In other words, keeping one's eyes open, faithfully applying oneself, and using one's head will help.

There may be some type of healing going on – perhaps around a creative friend or companion — and the door could be closing on that past hurt. This issue is not the main thing on the client's mind. I would mention it and see if they wanted to elaborate.

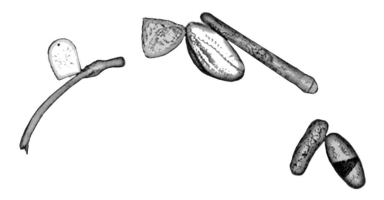

This group contains the Child Bead at the top left (play), the Possum Rib with a healed fracture below it (something that has healed). Next to that we have the Top Shell (an older person, late 60s or older), the Snake Head Cowrie Shell (a younger adult in their early 20s to 30s), and a Sea Anemone Spine (divider or pointer). The Master Root is below the Spine (mastery and skill) and the Lingam Stone is touching it (balance).

The Child Bead (play) and Possum Rib (something healed) could indicate that some recreation or relaxation has been, or could be, beneficial. The Top Shell (elderly person) and Snake Head Cowrie (young adult) could be people who will have an impact on the issue. The Master Root (mastery) and Lingam Stone (balance) could indicate the need for balance and mastery. The two people in this group might contribute in one or both areas. Dialogue with the client may provide more clarity here.

The circled and numbered pieces (next page) are away from the main body of the reading or isolated in relation to the other bones. You can choose to ignore these pieces or you can interpret them as they are, in isolation. A colleague who uses astrology for divination likens such pieces to "unaspected planets," which may reveal a powerful absence worthy of note in the reading.

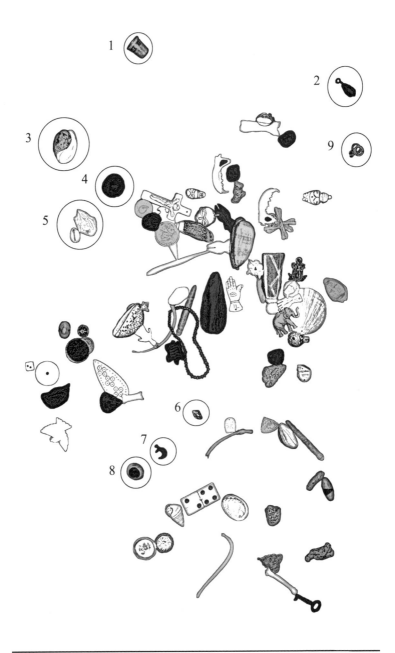

1. **Thimble (work):** The reading was about the client's business and the piece representing work is far removed from what is going on around the client and around the Rainbow Shell for "Now." This suggests that the client's real concern is something else that hasn't been mentioned. This happens more often than you would think. It could also be interpreted as the client not paying attention to his or her work because due to preoccupation with other issues closer to the Client Piece in the throw. Since we are looking at a business issue, the Thimble is worth noting to the client.

2. **Fishing Weight (a burden or heavy load):** I would ignore this piece. It is far from the client and not close enough to anything else to put it in any context.

3. **Bubble Shell (mother or maternal line):** This piece also seems to be of little relevance to this topic.

4. **Buckeye Nut (health):** In this throw the smooth side is showing which can be interpreted as no health issues or none that impact this issue. If the other side was showing I might ask if any health issues could be impacting the business.

5. **Purple Cowrie (a child) and Queen Elizabeth Root (feminine energy or issues):** Together these could indicate a female child or teenager and you could ask if there was such a person in the client's life. But even if the answer is yes, there doesn't seem to be much impact on the topic.

6. **Small Conch Shell (unborn baby, something that has been begun but has not come into fruition yet):** If this was near some other piece I would interpret it, but in this particular throw it doesn't have any context.

7. **Crescent Moon (New Moon):** I don't see where this piece would add to the reading either.

8. **Cat's Eye Shell (seeing clearly):** You could mention this or not. It does support the upright Domino.

9. **Handcuffs (being attached to something):** This piece also seems to have little impact on this reading.

The number 2 on the Die indicates to me that the reading is about a choice, and several areas lend themselves to choosing. The most obvious is the discrepancy between the stated concern for the business and the disinterest shown in the placement of the piece representing work. Choices will have to be made about how to constrict things, how to stay within the rules, whether to make a trip. Throughout your dialogue with the client you will be describing what you see. The client will have to decide what, if anything, to do about what you are seeing in the bones.

As to whether someone was working against the client using spiritual means, the reading does indicate some negativity not generated by a specific person. It also gives a recommendation for overcoming it. Had it not, I would have looked to see what was closest to the piece that represents ritual. I might also have done a separate throw, specifically asking for the best course of action. This throw could be of the whole set, or just the elements (earth, air, fire, and water), plus the Client Piece and Goddess Piece (ritual).

This sample was done in a somewhat orderly fashion. Real life can be far messier. While reading the throw by group order is possible, impromptu questions from the client often have you looking for a specific piece and what is going on around it, or you will go back to a previously interpreted grouping as more is subsequently revealed either by other bones or by the client.

SAMPLE READING 2
Relationship Reading

This is a short reading done for one my favorite clients. It was one throw of four in an hour-long reading; consequently emphasis was placed on the main point that applied to this specific question. She had broken up with a partner and although they had had no recent contact, she was still thinking of him. She wanted to know where they stood right now.

We will start with the Client Piece. The client is "standing on" the Lapis Lazuli Stone that represents water (emotions). Under that is a divider that gives the impression that the Lapis is wedged between it and the client's feet. This could be interpreted as the client stuffing down her emotions – keeping them tightly tamped down. The Skull piece is below the divider, which suggests it is not a part of this group. It will be read as part of another grouping.

Looking ahead, we see that the Woman (gratitude) lays over the Full Moon (things coming to an apogee).

The Arabic Cowrie that represents home is touching both the Full Moon and the Ring (relationships) and is also near to the face down Mirror (introspection).

Perhaps the client should be grateful for the fullness of her life and what she has –

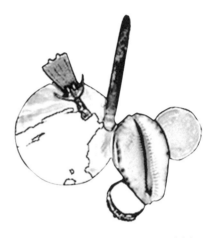

including relationships at home. The Mirror face down could be read as silent or may indicate that less introspection and more attention on the nearby pieces would be helpful.

Here we have the Ethiopian Protection Pendant face down (negative energy). It is covered by the Button (connection) which is touching the Copper Nugget (healing in progress).

Also touching the pendant is the Master Root (mastery) which is touching the Doll Head (a helpful spirit). This could be interpreted as telling the client that her healing is connected to allowing herself to feel those negative feelings and that she would have spiritual help and mastery over them if she did so.

Looking at the relationship (circled pieces 1 and 2 in the main drawing), you can see that they are pretty far apart. They are also both face down and behind the client in orientation. It looks like they are finished. Yet if you look at the bottom piece which I set as the client in the relationship the Head Piece (thoughts) is touching it and it is face down.

This could be interpreted as the client not thinking about the partner, but since she is paying for a reading about it, that is obviously not the case. It could then be interpreted as the client turning her mind away from the partner by will. The nearby Thimble (work) may indicate that it is requiring some effort. This also goes along with the client stepping on her emotions.

This group has the Domino face down (unaware, in denial), the Penny (small amount of money), the Crucifix face up (sacrifice), the Rough Stone (obstacle) on its back, the Snake Vertebra (backbone, strength), and a middle aged person whose sex is undetermined because there is no indication nearby.

The Domino indicates that the client is not facing emotions around the break-up. She may come into a small amount of money (heads-up Penny) or she may have funds available to her, but she will face obstacles and sacrifice. That the obstacle is touching and seems to be balanced on the Snake Vertebra could indicate that she will have to be strong but that she will be able to bear the difficulties ahead. A middle aged person may be involved and discussion with the client can shed more light on who this could be.

These groups are closest to the Client Piece and therefore most germane. Going further out we get into groups that are probably less important to the issue at hand.

This group is over the Client Piece's head. It has the Mask face down (secrets and things hidden), the Bowl open side up (need) over the Bird face down (messages from spirit or ancestors).

The Little John Root is nearby as is the Tiny Conch Shell (something that has not come into being yet).

The Mole Cowrie (ancient ancestors) and the Bubble Shell (mother or maternal side of the family) are also in this group, both face down.

Nothing seems to be hidden from the client and none of her ancestors seem to have anything to say. I would probably not say much about this group other than that.

This group contains the Rainbow Shell (now) piece on the far right, the Abalone Shell that shows what strengths the client brings to the situation, the Yin Yang bead (good fortune), the Child Piece face down (play), and Hamsa Hand #1, eye showing.

The way these pieces fell seems somewhat disorganized and disconnected. The "Now" piece seems somewhat detached indicating that perhaps the client is not fully in the present. The client has good fortune and spiritual help as her strengths right now. Those are good, but the client may not be feeling that way. Bringing them to her attention may be helpful.

The Die shows the number 2, which indicates that the reading is about a choice. Perhaps the client has been thinking about rekindling this relationship and about what it would entail. Discussion with the client would shed light on this.

The Garnet Bracelet (action) surrounding the Cat's Eye Shell (seeing clearly) face down. This is interesting in that it seems to be telling the client to not look! You could take it literally and advise the client not to look at this relationship – it is pretty much finished. But further discussion with the client could  shed more light on this. Perhaps the client has something more important going on that needs her full attention right now and daydreaming about an already finished relationship is a distraction she doesn't need at this time.

 Here we have the Heart (love) face up covered by the Frog (transformation) face down, covered by the Sacagawea Dollar (a significant sum of money). Nearby is the Possum Rib with the healed break (something that has healed) and the Diamond (look here, important).

This could be read as having something to do with love that results in a large sum of money. The Possum Rib suggests a healing around this, although it could be read as something separate from this grouping as well. Discussion with the client could shed further light on this.

This group is rather large, but all of the pieces are touching which at first glance suggests they should be read together. However, making a coherent narrative from these pieces would

be difficult to do in a short or even long reading so let's break it down into more manageable groups and pieces.

The Tiger Bell (warning) is face down indicating that there is nothing here that could be detrimental to the client.

The Snake Head Cowrie (an adult) is laying on the Silver Cowrie Coin (a medium amount of money) and is touching the Fishing Weight (a burden). This could be interpreted as an adult who brings money but with strings attached. There is not a lot of information here as to the  gender of the adult involved or the circumstances.

The next group has the Purple Cowrie (child) at the top. At bottom the Cougar Bone (solitude, isolation, and independence), is touching the Hamsa Hand #2 palm down (giving). It is joined to this group by the Mink Jaw face down (not speaking) over the Coyote Baculum (not speaking). The Mink Jaw is also touching the Birthing Woman Pendant (creativity, gratitude) not speaking.

The Birthing Woman (creativity) is covered by both the Nutmeg (luck) and the John the Conqueror Root (power and masculine energy). Topping this off is the Elephant (road opening, breaking past obstacles).

This could be read as an issue that can only be overcome with both good luck and power. It looks like it could involve a child and the client will probably be dealing with the situation without external help.

Here we have the stone that represents the earth, and the Silver Cowrie covered by the Olive Shell (the paternal line).

This could be interpreted as the father or a paternal ancestor being a good friend and someone the client can turn to for nurturing and physical or financial help.

The Arrow (things moving quickly), the New Moon (things happening but not seen), and the Lion Bone (courage, pride) are together and also touching this group.

This could be interpreted as the situation moving quickly, perhaps at the time of the New Moon (or the situation could herald a new beginning) and the client will need courage or feel proud of herself for how she handles a somewhat difficult situation.

As you see there was a lot of information in this large grouping and you could easily spend ten or fifteen minutes on it alone, but in a fifteen-minute reading, I would use the Tiger Bell as my cue and would most likely not mention most of what is contained here because it does not seem to have any bearing on the subject – the status of her relationship with her ex-partner. The operative word is "seem." That the pieces fell this way in response to the question indicates that it has some relevance.

However, in a short reading you have to decide what is most relevant to the client's question. If this were an hour long reading on this topic obviously this entire grouping would be one to explore with the client, perhaps in depth. Or the client may say that this doesn't ring true for them – they are not involved with any children or young people and do not anticipate any involvement in the future. If that is the case once you have interpreted this group you could move on to other topics.

This group is under the divider that the client is standing on. We have the Skull (ancestors or spirits), White Stone (history, memory, and stories), the Citrine (air, the intellect), the Carnelian (fire, passion). The Shoe is also here, but it is face down.

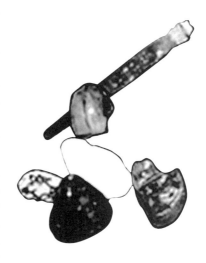

This could be interpreted as the client's ancestors and spirits are all supporting her mentally, passionately, and with stories and history. This is a strong foundation under the client and the bones were clear that this is what she is really standing on – her stamping down her feelings is a separate issue. This is a positive and uplifting message for the client.

The Mink Jaw (positive talk) covered by the Goddess (ritual) and the Doll Arm (help, assistance). This group is behind the Client. Perhaps some type of positive talk was helpful. In the context of ritual this could be affirmations, or prayer, or even counseling of some type. Again it is behind the Client Piece and doesn't add to the subject. In a short reading I would most likely not mention it.

This is a good place to speak about the Goddess or ritual piece for a bit. Ritual, as I interpret this piece, can be anything from saying an affirmation to a more elaborate ritual involving altars, spiritual bathing, and offerings in nature. I have found that if spirit speaks to me of a ritual for a client it is usually appropriate and well received by them.

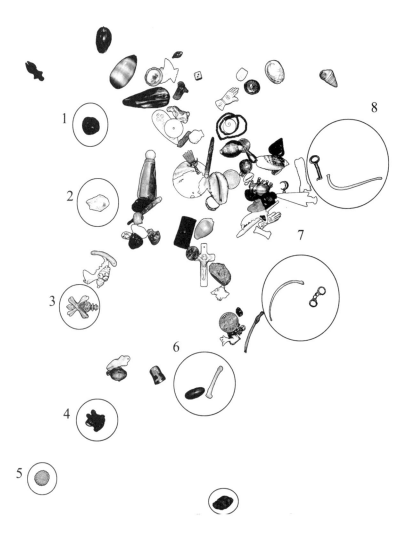

Remaining Bones

1. **Buckeye Nut (health):** Has the stem side up, indicating a possible health issue but it is behind the client.
2. **Queen Elizabeth Root (female energy):** Could be feeling a loss of femininity which is understandable when ending a relationship, but it is also behind the client.
3. **Skull and Crossbones (fear):** Behind the client.
4. **Turtle (things moving slowly):** Too far and out of context.
5. **Spinning Top Shell (elderly person):** Too far from the action.
6. **Lingam Stone (balance) and Dog Bone (faithful companion):** Too far from the action.
7. **Handcuffs (attachment) and Snake Rib (constriction):** Too far from the action
8. **Key (a door opening or closing) and Raccoon Baculum (a faithful man):** – too far from the action.

This reading took approximately 15 minutes so choices had to be made as to what was most important to the client's question. Things deemed less important were not covered or just mentioned in passing.

If you have a larger set like this one you have to learn to quickly identify the main points in the reading because most clients who want an hour long reading want to cover several topics. With a set this size you could easily spend an hour on one topic and still not cover all of the bones in the reading.

Both of the sample readings are interpreted here "as is," meaning that I am providing possible interpretations from an intellectual point of view with no guidance from the ancestors. What is written here is somewhat different from what I told the clients while reading for them. During the actual reading I was in a different mental space, open to and receiving guidance, and I was in dialogue with the client, providing amplifying information which I choose not to share here.

SAMPLE READING 3
Quick Daily Reading

Some people like to do a quick daily divination to start the day. Bones can be used for this purpose. I sit at my altar and calm my mind first. Then I call on God and the ancestors and throw. I don't read all of the bones or even every group of bone for this type of reading. Instead I pay attention to a few pieces of major importance:
- **The Client Piece (Raku Figurine)**
- **The "Now" Piece (Rainbow Shell)**
- **The Action Piece (Garnet Bracelet)**
- **The "Look Here" Piece (Diamond)**
- **The Gifts Piece (Abalone Shell)**

By looking at just these pieces I can get a good feel for what to expect for the day, what I should pay attention to, and the tools I have to accomplish what needs to be done. This sample is an actual reading I threw for myself on a routine day. I planned to meet a friend in the afternoon and go to the beach.

You don't have to use these pieces. You can use any pieces in your set that you feel are appropriate. You can even add a piece just for this purpose. If you haven't added any pieces, most of the available sets for purchase come with a Key. This will work well too — just explain what you are doing to your ancestors so that you are all working with the same set of symbols.

It could be useful to record these readings in a journal in the morning and then compare what you wrote with the events of the day. This may show you meanings for the pieces that fell for that day that you hadn't previously thought of. This will enhance your vocabulary of meanings and add subtlety and refinement to your interpretations. It will also increase your confidence in your ability to interpret as you find that your morning interpretations actually play out during the day. Plus it is an easy, low stress way to practice your skills on a regular basis.

First I looked at the Client Piece, which in this case represents me. There are a lot of pieces touching and nearby, specifically:

1. **Top Shell (elderly person).**
2. **Money Cowrie Shell (middle aged person).**
3. **Head (thoughts).**
4. **Goddess (ritual).**
5. **Tiny Conch Shell (unborn baby).**
6. **Unidentified Rough Stone (obstacle).**
7. **Thimble (work).**
8. **Rainbow Shell ("Now").**
9. **Fishing Weight (a burden).**
10. **Master Root (mastery).**
11. **Relationship Piece (one of the two Relationship Pieces).**

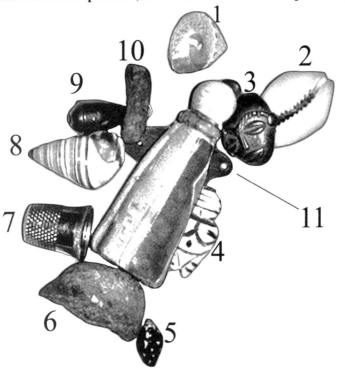

The Client Piece is laying on top of the Relationship Piece (11). If I read this as my spouse, I can see I may be relying on him or at least need his help today. The Head (3) is right near my head, which I would interpret as my being focused. It is also touching the Money Cowrie representing a middle aged person (2). This could be me or it could be someone else. The Goddess (ritual) Piece (4) is also touching me, which makes sense because I will be meeting with someone today for just that purpose! I appear to be standing on the Rough Stone (obstacle) Piece (6) and it is touching the Unborn Baby (5). I may be facing obstacles today but the Client Piece seems to be on the way to a new idea or plan.

The Thimble (work) Piece (7) is also touching me, but I seem to be moving away from it. Again, this fits, as I will be doing some work on a project in the morning and heading out with my friend in the afternoon. The Rainbow Shell ("Now") Piece (8) just adds to the feel of this being what is going on right this minute. If it were somewhere else on the cloth I would interpret it and the pieces around it as what is likely to happen today.

The Fishing Weight (burden) (9) is also right behind me. It is covered by the Master Root (mastery) (10). I would interpret this as my leaving my burdens behind for the day — mastering them perhaps. Finally the Top Shell (an elderly person) (1) may be on my mind or may have some impact on my day. The placement could indicate it is in the back of my mind. This would fit for my mother, who is in good health, but is still of an age that I worry about her. I debated even including it in this reading as it is not touching me. The Diamond (bottom left)  tells me of something important for the day. It is not close to any other pieces, but I included the two closest pieces just the same. The Turtle says that I should move slowly and deliberately and the Elephant says that obstacles will be removed.

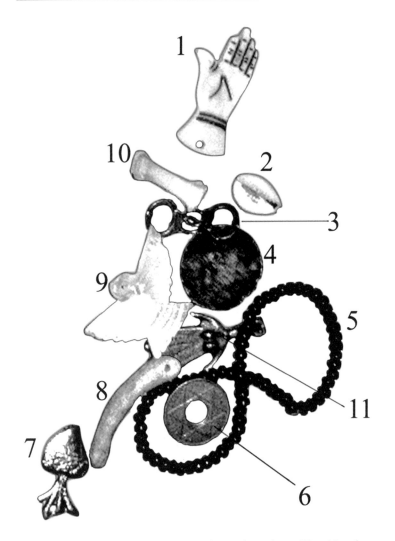

Here we have the Garnet Bracelet action piece (5) with a large group of pieces around it. Again, I could have excluded the pieces on the periphery of this group to save time if I were in a hurry. Each case is a judgment call and you should rely on your ancestors and spirits to make the right call.

1. Hamsa Hand #1, palm side up (requesting spiritual help)
2. Small Cowrie Shell (child)
3. Handcuffs (attachment)
4. Mirror, face up (introspection)
5. Bracelet (action)
6. Coin (medium amount of money)
7. Heart (emotions)
8. Doll Arm (help from a spirit)
9. Shell Bird (message from a spirit)
10. Cougar Bone (walking alone, grace)
11. Woman (gratitude)

The first place I look here is to see what is in the Bracelet (action) piece. The Coin could be telling me to take action around finances today. The Woman (gratitude) is also there. Being thankful will be another action for the day. The Doll Arm (help) and Mother of Pearl Bird (spiritual message) are touching the gratitude piece and it is close to the Heart. I will be on the lookout for messages and help from the spirits today. The Cougar Bone, Handcuffs, and Mirror seem to be telling me to make time for introspection and self-care.

Hamsa Hand #1 is a bit further away from the action piece, but I have two other spirit-related pieces in this group, so I decided to include it. It tells me to ask for spiritual help. The Child Piece does not seem to make sense here. I do not interact much with children, but it may mean that I am the child here — that spirit wants to help me and all I need do is ask. A powerful message for me today.

The Abalone Shell represents gifts that I bring to the situation.

 The closest piece to it is the Child Piece that represents play. I see this as a reminder to not get too bogged down in the serious topics of the day — the obstacles, the finances, looking for and requesting spiritual help, and all of the other things swirling around me for the day. My good humor and sense of fun will help me get through what looks like a busy day.

As it turns out this reading was pretty much spot on in everything it said. I spent part of the day working hard on a project and the latter part out in nature where ritual was done. While it takes a while to read and follow here, in practice it should only take a few minutes to look at the focal points and form some impressions.

SAMPLE READING 4
Can I Increase My Income?

The client has recently started a home business doing psychic readings and rootwork and wishes to know how to increase her income without increasing the number of days she is available to the public. The client has another income-producing business which precludes her from working on the new business full time. She has been in business approximately six months and feels that

the business seems not to be growing. She states her income from the business is good some months and not so good other months and wishes to know whether her expectations are unreasonable and how she can achieve a better income over time.

First let's look at the Client Piece, which is standing on the Unborn Baby (an idea not yet brought to fruition). The Rainbow Shell ("Now") is nearby. Perhaps the client has some ideas on how to improve her income already – she just hasn't done anything about them. She seems to be standing on them or keeping them down for a reason not revealed. Discussion with the client could shed some light on this.

The Arabic Cowrie (home) and Skull (a spirit) are overhead. This suggests that the client's home has spiritual protection.

This large group has been chosen together because the pieces all cluster around the Diamond (look here), indicating an area of special interest to the client.

Starting at the upper left we find the Hamsa Hand #2, the giving hand, the Crucifix, blessings side up, and Yin Yang (good fortune). This could indicate that the client should be generous where possible because to do so will bring good fortune. Perhaps the client can donate some readings or rootwork to those in need who do not have the financial resources to hire her. This is followed by the Bubble Shell (the maternal line), the Top Shell (an elderly person), the Olive Shell (the paternal line), and the Elephant, which knocks down obstacles.

Are the client's parents involved in the business somehow? Perhaps they loaned the client money to start the business, answer phones, manage shipping, provide childcare, or are otherwise involved in some way.

If this is not the case I would go on to the next two pieces – the Citrine (the element air) and the John the Conqueror Root (power). Intellect, personal strength, and power could be qualities the client has inherited from the parents. That they are near the Diamond (pay attention), which is above them, indicates that these traits will be important to the client's success in this venture. These pieces seem to be reassuring the client that she has the qualities she needs already.

The Diamond is next, followed by the Green Aventurine (the element earth), touching the face-up Mask (secrets). The Mask is also touching the face-down Cat's Eye (reusing to see), further reinforcing that there is something that the client is not seeing. The Button (connection) is also touching the Mask. What can this combination mean? Something is hidden or not being looked at connected to earth which is material, and practical. If the earth piece were a Coin I would think that the client should look closely at the financial aspects of the business. But earth encompasses finances and much more. I would likely interpret this as the client perhaps not being realistic or practical in her expectations. Further pieces may shed more light on this.

Here we have the Crescent Moon or New Moon (unseen actions), the Sacagawea Dollar Coin face up, indicating a large sum of cash, and the Master Root (mastery) together. This could indicate that financial rewards will come with mastery. The New Moon implies that it may be happening without being visible. This could mean that the client's income will go up with experience and additional training to hone her skills.

The Dog Bone (loyal companion), the Nutmeg (luck), the Thimble (work), the Handcuffs (attachment) and the Penny (small amount of money) face down are also in this group. I would read this as saying faithful efforts and perhaps a small expenditure of some sort will result in luck or a change in luck for the client. But these things are all connected. The client will have to work and invest in the business faithfully to make her own luck.

This group as a whole seems to be telling the client that she will have to continue to hone her skills, gain experience, invest some small amount of money, and be faithful to applying these steps if she hopes to reap the financial rewards she is seeking. The financial rewards could be significant if she does so, even if it doesn't seem like progress is being made at first (New Moon).

Here we have the Mink Jaw (positive speech and good repute). Under it is the Head, face down, so not speaking, the Domino, face up (the client is aware), covered by the creativity of the Birthing Woman.

The Arrow (far away events or quick changes) is beneath the face-up Domino and Full Moon (apogee). The Spine separates this group from the previous group.

The Mink Jaw speaks for itself – people speak well of the client and she enjoys a good reputation. There are a couple of ways we could interpret the remaining pieces. We could choose to only read the top two pieces – the Full Moon and creativity. Perhaps the client will bring a creative project into fruition around the Full Moon as an actual time period. Perhaps it is the symbol of the culmination of her creative efforts rather than a time period. That she is standing on an idea (the Unborn Baby under the Client Piece's feet) gives support to this interpretation and suggests that she should pursue this idea.

We could also choose to read the Domino and Arrow as part of this group. The Domino being face up indicates that the client is aware of what is going on with the subject of the reading. The Arrow is interesting though. In its current placement it could be seen as being held down by the Full Moon. This could mean that things may start to move more quickly once the Full Moon (the culmination of the creative idea) passes.

 This small group has the Carnelian (the element fire) under the Ring (relationships) and the Heart (emotions). Obviously the client loves this work and is passionate about what she is doing, which is pretty typical of people doing spiritual work.

Here we have the Coyote Baculum, the healed Possum Rib, and the Skeleton Key, indicating possible betrayal, something that has healed, and a door opening or closing. These are near one of the Couple Pieces face down, and the Goddess (a ritual), face down.

After this we have the Coprolite (elements of the past best left behind) and the Abalone Shell (gifts the client brings to the situation). This is an interesting group and the Coprolite, healed Possum Rib, Coyote Baculum and Key all seem to be working together as the gifts the client brings. This could be some previous unpleasant event or betrayal or some difficult painful period where the client was really struggling to get by. Perhaps she has closed the door on it or put behind her, but that experience could be helpful here.

I would ask the client about this. Perhaps she has had a previous business experience in which she learned a hard lesson that would be useful here. Usually I interpret Coprolite as old experiences that we are still carrying with us to our detriment, but in this case it appears to be a strength.

We also have the Turtle on its back (silent), the Bird face down (silent), the Silver Cowrie (a good friend) and the beaded Garnet Bracelet (action to be taken). These pieces are close enough to the Abalone Shell (the client's gifts) to be interpreted with it.

Perhaps the client has good friends she can count on – another gift she brings to the situation. The Turtle on its back could be interpreted as being silent or as the client feeling like she is struggling hard but getting nowhere. Given the other pieces so far, I would most likely read it as silent. The client has not indicated that she is struggling in any way.

The Garnet Bracelet or action piece is empty. That indicates that there is no specific or particular thing the client should do to reach her goal. I might recommend that she follow the advice given earlier about investing time and money into honing her skills.

This is another interesting group. We have the Ethiopian Eye Pendant face down over the Coin representing a medium amount of money. The Eye Pendant is touching the Lion Bone which is under the Raccoon Baculum. Nearby are the Snake Vertebra and the Purple Top Cowrie representing a child. Backbone, courage, faithful protection, and care touching possible enemy work or negative energy. This work or energy is holding down money. This could suggest that someone, most likely a competitor, is working against the client. Her strength and other positive qualities may have been able to minimize the damage, but if the work were counteracted this could free up the client's earning capability.

I might ask the client about the Child Piece. It could be saying that the client has been strong or brave because of a child, but it is unlikely a child has much bearing on the client's subject and if she answered in the negative I would move on.

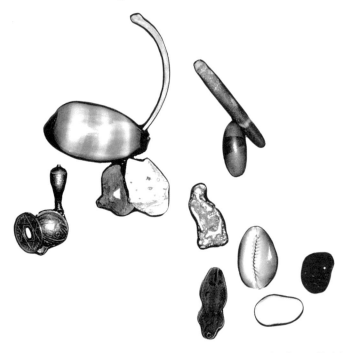

Starting on the left we have a Star of David Coin from British West Africa (a medium amount of money) on the Tiger Bell which is warning side down, and the Fishing Weight. This extra coin got into the set by accident, but since it is here I will use it. This small group could be saying that uncertainty (the Coin is on edge) is becoming a weight on the client's shoulders.

Next we have the Mole Cowrie (ancient ancestors) with the Snake Rib and the Queen Elizabeth Root (female energy) This could mean that ancient female ancestors support the client's work in this area.

The Little John to Chew Root (law or rules) is touching the Mole Cowrie and Queen Elizabeth Root. The Copper Nugget (healing) and Lingam Stone (balance) are also nearby, as is the Snake Head Cowrie (a young adult), the White Howlite Stone (stories or history) and the Lapis Lazuli representing the element water. The second Couple Piece is here, face down (silent), as is a Spine (divider).

I would be tempted to take these all as descriptive of the ancestor who is providing support to the client. Female, involved with law or rules (a priestess or judge?), involved with healing and balance, in her prime when she became an ancestor, who worked with history, stories, and water.

You could also separate this out into the pieces touching the ancestor and apply the others to the young adult, asking the client if this sounded like anyone she knew. This is a group where your ancestors and spirits are so important because you will often know which way to interpret with their help.

Starting from the top we have a small group with the open Bowl (need) atop the Frog, which is on its back and so silent, and the Doll Head (a helpful spirit). The message here is that the client needs help from the spirit world.

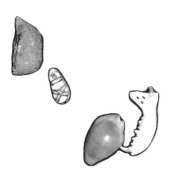

The Shoe is near the Rough Obstacle Stone. Travel could be an obstacle of some sort, but earlier we saw the means of knocking down obstacles is close to the client and her parents. Perhaps her parents will be able to help her make any necessary trips. Finally we have the Money Cowrie, a middle aged person, bitten by the Mink Jaw, speaking ill of the client or spreading gossip. I would point this out. The client may already know or have a good idea who this could be.

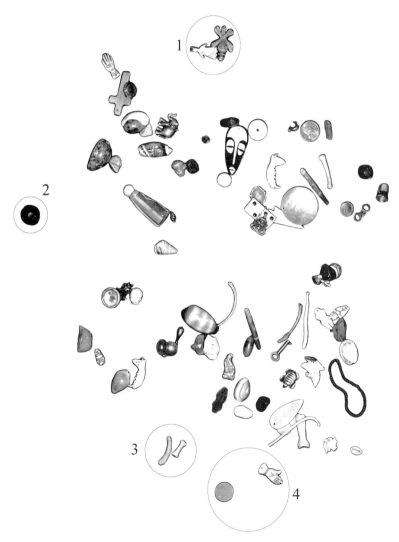

The circled pieces have not yet been addressed. They are on the outer edges of the throw and somewhat isolated so they are likely less important. At position 1 we have the Woman (gratitude) face down and the Skull and Crossbones (fear) face up.

They are rather removed from the client or the present so while there may be some fear, it is not a major factor here.

Position 2 has the Buckeye Nut (health) with the smooth side up which suggests there are no health issues or that health issues are not a factor in this issue.

Position 3 is the Doll Arm and the Cougar Bone – walking alone, being independent but with help available should she desire it.

Position 4 is the Mirror face down and Hamsa Hand #1 (spiritual help), which is open suggesting that she is or will receive help from the spirits and ancestors. These pieces are also far from the main action. It is never a mistake to seek help from one's ancestors and spirits so you could mention this to the client, but previous groups have addressed this issue in more detail.

Finally, two pieces landed outside of the reading surface during the throw – the Die showing the number three (things are flowing smoothly) and the Child Piece (play). These two pieces did not wish to speak during the reading.

You could just leave it at that or you could interpret the pieces which left the reading surface as indicating that there is no place for play and that a smooth flow of events is not important. Rather, the client needs to take things seriously as she is offering services that can have real effects on people's lives.

While this reading did not reveal a specific action the client could take to increase and steady her earnings, it did provide a wealth of information that the client found useful and affirming of her own instincts on the matter and she left feeling that she was on the right track and just needed to be more patient. She indicated that she would consider further training, as suggested.

CONCLUSION

Hopefully this book has given you some ideas for putting your own set of bones together and reading them.

I want to emphasize again that the ancestor work is an integral piece of this system. Read through the ancestors and your spirits and thank them for their help and assistance.

My feeling is that our secular society has lost an important part of itself because we are so focused on "us" and "now." Honoring and remembering our ancestors would go a long ways into helping us to honor and respect ourselves and others. Keeping in mind that one day we too may be ancestors may help us to act in ways that would make our descendants proud.

I feel that the ancestors and spirit are making themselves more noticeable in our world today. By means of our ability to instantly communicate with each other, we now have easy access to information about our ancestors and about various methods to work with and honor them. Bone reading can be one of those methods. I have found it to be both spiritual and practical and my hope is that you will too.

Happy Bone Reading!

SOURCES

BONE READING SETS

Lucky Mojo Curio Company
6632 Covey Road, Forestville, California 95436
voice: 707-887-1521 / fax: 707-887-7128
email: order@luckymojo.com / LuckyMojo.com
Lucky Mojo was the first U.S. company I am aware of that put bone reading sets together for sale. Their sets contain 21 pieces, which can vary due to availability, and a two page instruction sheet. They published cat yronwode's *Throwing the Bones* and they also carry animal bones, shells, amulets, and curios of many kinds.

ConjureDoctor.com Home of Dr. E. products
ConjureDoctor.com
Dr. E. has joined the ancestors, but his family now runs his business and continues to supply products and services. You can get Lucky Mojo Sangoma-Style Bone Reading Sets from them.

The Mystic Dream
1437 N Broadway, Walnut Creek, California 94596
925-933-2342
TheMysticDream.com
The Mystic Dream sells Bone Reading Sets containing 15 pieces. The pieces may vary due to availability.

REAL ANIMAL BONES

The Bone Room: Natural History Store
1569 Solano Ave. Berkeley, California 94707
(510) 526-5252
BoneRoom.com

The Bone Room has a large variety of animal bones and other items that can be used in a bone reading set. They are a good source to try if you are looking for a bone from a particular species of animal. If you don't see what you want on their website, call their shop because the site only lists a small portion of their inventory.

The Evolution Store
120 Spring St. N.Y., N.Y.
TheEvolutionStore.com
The Evolution Store has a good assortment of animal bones and other curios and you can order online.

Skulls Unlimited International
SkullsUnlimited.com
1-800-659-7585
An online retailer with a large assortment of animal bones.

FURTHER READING

catherine yronwode, *Throwing the Bones: How to Foretell the Future with Bones, Shells, and Nuts*, Lucky Mojo, 2012.
This book is an excellent introduction to various methods of sortilege and intuitive bone reading from around the world.

Mama Starr, *Read'en Dem Conjure Bones*, Old Style Conjure, 2013.
Starr demonstrates what she calls a "traditional conjure bone reading" as she was taught, modified slightly for ease of learning.

Philip M. Peek, editor, *African Divination Systems: Ways of Knowing*. Indiana University Press, 1991.
An academic work by various authors describing divination methods in several African cultures.

Ulufudu, *The Zulu Bone Oracle*. Wingbow Press, 1989.
This book describes a system adapted from the Zulu culture and incorporating Zulu numerology.

Claire O'Neill, *The Oracle of the Bones*. St. Martin's Press, 1994.
This book is part of a set that has four replica bones and a cloth to be used as a reading surface. Although the number of bones is small, their design is such that there are several ways they can fall, thus creating many interpretive possibilities.

Raven Whitehorse, *Stones, Bones, and Totems*. Around Townes Publishing, 2013.
The author has a set of bones that she has gathered over many years. From her bone reading system, she has created a divination deck, allowing you to carry it with you.

Henri A. Junod, *The Life of a South African Tribe*. Imprimerie Attinger Freres, 1913.
Volume II of this set has a section on the bone reading of the Thonga tribe of South Africa. It gives a fairly detailed description of the bones used, their meanings, and the method of divination, with photographs and line drawings of bone sets and actual readings.

John Matthews, editor, *The World Atlas of Divination*. Little, Brown and Company, 1992.
Has a short overview on bone reading as performed by several tribes in South Africa.

Susan Schuster Campbell, *Spirit of the Ancestors: Lessons from Africa*. Lotus Press, 2002.
This book provides a simple means for working with your ancestors and several anecdotes of the role the ancestors play in our lives. Although she was a student of P.H. Mtshali, a South African sangoma, the material provided is secular.

Alodokun, *Ancestor Paths: Honoring Our Ancestors and Guardian Spirits Through Prayers, Rituals, and Offerings, a Step by Step Guide*. Oba Ilari Aladokun, 2009.

This book provides information on working with your ancestors from a Lukumi / Santeria / Ifa / Espiritismo perspective, adapted so that anyone can work with the information.

MY TEACHERS

Chas Bogan — Chas did the reading for me that started it all. He is one of the co-proprietors of The Mystic Dream and teaches classes there from time to time.

cat yronwode — I bought my first set of bones at the Lucky Mojo Curio Company and cat, a longtime friend, was kind enough to spend some time give me many tips and pointers.

Gretchen Crilly McKay — Gretchen is an initiated sangoma and shaman. She is an amazing teacher and human being and she can be reached at her website AncestralWisdom.com

Every bone reader who was kind enough to swap a reading with me was also one of my teachers, as are my clients, and the folks who come to my workshops and classes.